Who You Are

Who You Are

Defying the Circumstances
that Define Us

JOHN CROYLE

Founder of  *Big Oak Ranch*

B&H
PUBLISHING GROUP
NASHVILLE, TENNESSEE

Dedication

To everyone who is still looking to finally find
that person you really are and were designed to be.

Contents

INTRODUCTION

Who Are You?

I don't know who you are.

In fact, I'd be willing to bet that few people in your life really know who you are, even the ones who think they know you the best. But if I were guessing, I'd say the person you really are is probably not entirely the person you want to be. Is that about right?

That's because nearly every one of us comes from a broken place of some kind, places we'd just as soon not talk about. Places that have left us with struggles we don't even want to admit we're dealing with. Failures we're still trying to dig our way out of. And even if that's not so true of you—even if you weren't broken too badly from the start—I think it's fair to say we've all done a pretty good job of breaking a whole bunch of stuff along the way. Haven't we?

I know I sure have.

That makes you and me, when you get right down to it, not so fundamentally different from the hundreds, now couple of thousand kids who've done a lot of their growing up here at

Big Oak Ranch these past forty years. One after another they showed up on our doorstep . . .

Broken.

Broken a lot worse than you, I'd expect, in many ways. In horrible, *horrible* ways. But broken just the same.

Abused. Tortured. Mistreated. Belittled. Abandoned. Neglected. Scarred. And scared. Not what anybody wants to be. Especially not at six, ten, twelve, fifteen years old—barely getting started in life without really getting much of a shot at it yet.

No, it's not pretty. Never is. Some of the stories I could tell you—some of the ones you'll read about in these pages—unless you'd been here to see it, hear it, and feel it for yourself, no way could you possibly believe it. *Nobody* could.

And yet—

If you were to go with me today to the Westbrook Christian School where our kids attend, and we were to pass a handful of them in the hallway between lunch and fourth period . . .

Or if we were sitting outside waiting while a few of them were hiking back up from an early morning work detail at the chicken house or the cattle barn . . .

Or if a couple of them were shaking off, dripping wet from a squealing plunge into the lake or the swimming pool . . .

I'd put an arm around them, point my other hand in your direction, and I'd say to them, "Tell this man, tell this woman . . . tell them who you are."

I'm Sally, they'd say.

I'm Robby. I'm Samantha.

I'm Derek. Cindy. Travis. Mary.

They'd say it with their eyes looking square into yours. They'd say it with a nice, firm, full-arm-extended handshake. They'd say it where you could hear it, not mumbled into the ground, as if they could hardly care less about themselves, about you. They'd say it with a bright, confident smile. They'd say it with their head up, with their shoulders stout. They'd say it like they mean it.

They'd say it because that's who they *are*.

Not who they *were*.

And that's the cool thing about it—because it doesn't really matter what they've been. Or what *any* of us have been. Doesn't really matter that you've perhaps lived a lot of your life so far without doing everything you wanted to do, without being everything you wanted to be. End of the day, the person you've been in the past only gets permission to be who you *were*.

And I don't want you hung up on who you *were*. I want you starting fresh today with who you *are*. And who you're going to be tomorrow. And the next day. And the next day.

That's the person I'm talking to.

That's the person I'm interested in.

Because those are the people we've given our lives to help rescue and restore and introduce to you as poised, alert, well-spoken kids whose hearts—so badly broken—are now far, far along in the healing process. By the grace of God and the amazing work of many loving people, they are standing here today bursting at the seams with potential and hope.

Some of our kids, when they came to us, had been blistered on half their body with the business end of a burning cigarette. Some of our kids had been repeatedly raped by their mother's perverted boyfriend or by a sick-minded relative who saw them as nothing but a piece of worthless trash to toss in the corner, a toy for their devilish hatred. Some of our kids showed up here in wrinkled clothes they'd snatched from a parking lot Goodwill bin, just so they could find something decent to put on.

Trust me, I've seen it all.

And then some.

But I dare you, from taking even a studied look at any grouping of our kids today—to tell me which ones grew up being slapped in the head every day at home for no reason. Tell me which ones never knew for sure if there was going to be any supper on the table at night. Tell me which ones cycled from one rotten, rejecting home environment to the next—nobody ever wanting them, everybody telling them how much trouble they were, what a nuisance they caused, what somebody wouldn't give if they could just get rid of them. Which they ultimately did.

I guarantee, you couldn't tell the difference. You wouldn't know.

Because that's not who they are.

Not anymore.

The kids who live here with us are not bad kids. Oh, they've come to us from some mighty bad places. They've been in some bad circumstances. They've seen things and heard things and had to be afraid of things that most of us—even if we've seen people acting it out in the movies—cannot even begin to imagine the reality. Trembling in their beds. Afraid to go to sleep because of real—not imagined—monsters. Hiding scrapes and bruises from their friends. Staying away just to stay safe.

I know where every last one of these kids has come from. I know all their backstories, their family history. I know everything that happened to them that made them who they were. And none of it matters to me even *this much* in terms of the vision our whole organization, down to the last person, holds up to them for what they can become. Because as soon as they're ours—as soon as they're *our* kids—they're loved, they're provided for, they're grounded in responsibility. And they're promised a chance at life that nobody ever gave them before.

I'm sure you've seen those big, backlit maps in the shopping malls, the ones where a giant diagram of the whole place is exploded out in one view. The shoe store, it says, is over there; the sporting goods store is up a level around the corner; the food court is out in the middle somewhere. And you—*you,* the little arrow says—"You Are Here."

That's basically what I've been saying for forty years to every child we've received into our care. Every time they first come in and sit across the desk from me, I always make them the same four promises: (1) I love you. (2) I'll never lie to you. (3) I will stick with you until you're grown. And (4) there are boundaries; don't cross them. In other words, I know how things worked before (I tell them) in the environments where you've been. But listen to me: you aren't there anymore, understand? *You are here.* And now's the day when you can truly start becoming who you *are,* not be chained down for the rest of your life to who you *were.*

I promise you.

And in some ways, I guess, I'm making the same sort of promise to you today. I'm hoping, throughout the course of this book, as I sort of wind back through some of the many wonders God has performed down here on these gorgeous tracts of Alabama acreage, that you won't just hear an old guy telling his story for the millionth time because it's not really about me. Nor is it only about our kids, as wonderful and incredible and inspirational as they are. Nor is it only about the dedicated staff and houseparents who pour so much of themselves into this boundless task.

Truth is, I wouldn't be wasting a minute telling this story right now if I didn't think *you* were a part of it too.

We've seen God change literally hundreds of futures right here in front of our eyes. *Change?* I don't know if *change* is actually a good enough word for it. People can change a tire, change a lightbulb, change their shirt, change their order at the drive-through. What happens here at Big Oak Ranch is not just *change.* What happens here is . . .

To put it in football language, it's about like the difference between changing the first-down markers and changing the scoreboard. One's just another play; the other is six momentum-changing points that'll show up in the paper tomorrow, maybe even in big, bold print in the headlines.

I'm talking about *that* kind of change.

Game-changing change.

So, simply because of what I've already seen, I don't need to stretch my faith completely out of its skin to believe that God doesn't have big dreams and callings stirring around in your heart right now. Changes that He's still wanting to bring about *in* you, *through* you. Passions and pursuits that are meant to *push* you, no doubt, but more importantly to *place* you right in the stream of His blessing, where you're guaranteed to be more energized and fulfilled than you've ever been in your life.

Doing what He wants you to do, doing what He's *created* you to do—that's sure to get your blood pumping.

If you'll do it.

So sit down here, and let me just talk with you a little while about the kids and people and stories and—the miracles, really— that we've been privileged to watch and be part of at Big Oak Ranch. I'm so proud of these kids, and, as you'll see, I cannot say enough good about them. But I'm praying that, even if you walk away with just two or three memorable things that come out while we're visiting like this, those two or three moments will be all it takes to make you want to get up from here, shake the rust off your drive and your fighting spirit, and start going hard after some things you've maybe been avoiding, afraid of, or putting off.

Because if, like I said, you're not entirely satisfied with who you are, well—

You *can* be satisfied with what God would love to be doing through your life right now if you'd just get over who you've been, get on board with whatever you've been resisting, and get moving in the direction He's wanting to take you.

I'll stack up forty imperfect but incredible years against that promise . . . to prove I know what I'm talking about.

CHAPTER 1

Tag

You're It

 We had no other choice. We had to suspend the boy from school. Automatic.

That's the rule.

But that night I took him out for a nice steak dinner. Made sure they took really good care of him.

Because that's how proud I was of what he'd done.

When Curt first came to us, he was thirteen years old. A runaway from home. The stuff he'd seen, the stuff he'd been made to do—even a young kid finally reaches the point where he's just not going to be forced to do that mess anymore. Better off living on the streets, figuring it out himself, learning the ropes, getting by.

Fortunately one of the things he "got by" to do along the way was to show up and talk with *us*. And when he did, we

7

gladly took him in as our own. Curt's got a family now. A big one.

And he loves it.

So that's why, when he heard about a boy who'd been saying some inappropriate things to a few of our girls, making them feel uncomfortable and harassed at school, he went straight up to the guy and gave him what you might call a . . . let's say, a recommendation. "You need to quit talking to my sisters like that."

To which the other boy said something to the effect of, "And what are you going to do about it?"

In the two blurring seconds it took to raise that punk up over his head, Curt already realized he probably hadn't chosen the best way to handle the situation. As he told me later in my office—calmer by then, having had some time to give it a little twenty-twenty hindsight—"What I did was right; I just handled it wrong." Sounded like a pretty good postmortem analysis to me.

Postmortem. I don't mean by that he killed the boy, OK? We don't run that kind of school. But after pinning him down on the ground, clearly answering the "what are you going to do about it" question, Curt delivered again the same piece of advice he'd suggested a few moments earlier, only now with some added weight to his words, applied somewhere at about the other boy's sternum. Establishing communication.

"You don't understand, that's all the family I've got," he said, by way of rationale. "And I don't let anybody treat 'em that way."

I sure haven't heard of anybody talking ugly to those girls since.

Can't say I'm surprised, can you?

Now don't get the idea that Curt's one of those guys who goes around looking for trouble. He may indeed have the moves and muscle of a seasoned street fighter. But he's the kind of kid who, at seventeen—when I dropped him off at home recently—ran up to his housemom and gave her a big hug. Planted a kiss on her cheek. Right out there in front of God and everybody. She looked back at me from around his full embrace, waved, gave a little wink—the unspoken acknowledgment of our shared joy at watching a kid like this, treated like garbage for thirteen years of his young life, now able to give and express such unvarnished love.

"You could put me in the middle of downtown Harlem," that woman said to me one time, talking about Curt's loyalty to her, "and I'd be fine. Nobody would touch me."

Because Curt—he's got it.

It.

Listen, I see boys and girls here every day at the Ranch who've got "it"—a special something that elevates them above the sad conditions of their upbringing, an inner strength that is cementing them into people who know who they are and know where they intend to go. I've been watching it happen for years.

I'm not pretending now that every kid who's housed, fed, educated, and nurtured through our program turns into everything a parent could dream of—although, let's be real, neither does every kid on your street, in your subdivision, or in your church or school system . . . not by a *long* shot. Some of the most messed-up kids in the world come from "normal" families, where the dysfunction is no less real, just more easily and secretly disguised.

So are our kids perfect? No.

Are *we* perfect? *Shoot,* no.

But I know firsthand the various degrees of hell the children under our care have come from. And I've seen enough maturity, loyalty, courage, faith, compassion, grit, excellence, and hard work in them to know for sure that *it* can exist in anybody, anywhere.

Even in me. Even in you.

I believe God has put something inside all of us that—if we'll ever get over ourselves, if we'll ever start doing what we know to be right, if we'll ever quit being so afraid of what other people might think or say—we could uncork the kind of opportunities that would spin our lives into a whole new orbit. We'd be walking around not with insecure arrogance but with deep-rooted confidence. With eyes that aren't trained on the rearview mirror anymore, or even on the windshield, but way out there on the horizon where dreams live. We could operate with a passionate persistence that simply will not give up and after falling down—again and again and again—keeps getting up and lugging that wagon forward.

I believe God can transform us into people who put others first just as naturally as we always used to put *ourselves* first. People who realize we're better off being a tool in God's hand than telling Him what to do all the time. More giver than taker. More friend than critic. More bricklayer than excuse maker. We can be men and women who realize our own limitations, who know we're in need of a lot of help, but who also aren't sitting around waiting for people to coddle us and hold our hand. We're on. We're going. Expecting a headwind? Yes. But we're digging in for the long haul, building deep and sturdy.

And like I said, some of the people I've met and been around who exhibit these types of qualities the best are living right here today at Big Oak Ranch. Their age may quantify them as boys and girls, as teenagers, as high schoolers, but their character defines them as being more man or woman than a lot of the grown men and women I know.

Tragically, of course, some of what's pushed them so hard toward maturity has come from being made to grow up too fast. They've been introduced to certain dark aspects of life before most of us ever figured out how to tie our shoes or count by twos. In many instances they've been called upon to make wartime-level decisions in a second-grader's body. When a seven-year-old boy stands between his mom and her enraged boyfriend and tells him to stop hitting her, then takes the brunt of the blows himself from a man who outweighs him by 180 pounds, that little guy has stepped into Manhood 101 right then and there. Not that anybody's happy to think he ever faced that situation or wants to imagine what went through his head when without a moment's hesitation he jumped into the middle of a mismatch like that. Boys like this have taught me that real courage is not determined by age, especially when he told me, "Yeah, that guy beat me up pretty bad, but you know what?"

"What?"

"He didn't hit my mama any more."

MANHOOD, plain and simple.

And as we get started here, I just want you to know God is looking for men and women who will step up with that kind of conviction and say: "I'm here to defend the people I love. I'm here to say what I mean and stand by it no matter what it costs. I'm here to lead by the clout of my honesty and integrity, not by manufacturing an image of somebody I'm not. I'm here to serve and sacrifice and help and care, and *not* care about getting the credit."

God can do big things with people like that.

With people who are going after it.

With people who've got it.

You may be somebody who's already doing that, and as a result you're seeing the visible fruit of God's blessing on a regular basis. Or you may be somebody who did it that way once upon a time, but life has sort of taken the starch out of your energy and discipline. You've gotten tired, discouraged, decided to park it for a while. Or you may be somebody who really desires this kind of consistency and purpose and mission and calling, but things just seem to keep getting in your way, not the least of which is the unpredictable person whose picture is on your driver's license.

Or maybe you stumbled upon this book for whatever reason, primarily just interested to see what Big Oak is all about, what we do here, how we got here. You weren't really meaning for this to get personal. That's OK. I'm not going to preach at you. That's not my style. But I'm telling you, the story of Big

Oak Ranch at its heart is simply the story of what happens when God stirs "it" up inside of you.

He does things. He moves things. He brings people toward you. He gives you wisdom that couldn't possibly come out of your own ignorant head. He steadies you. He multiplies you. He hears you when you call out for help. And, boy, does He ever satisfy you.

He makes *who you are*—dings, dents, and all—into somebody He can use to make a difference. What else could we really want?

The Big Oak story is just one story. A good one, a cool one. But it's meant to be only one in a galaxy of millions.

And one of those stories is what God wants to do in you.

Come and Get It

One of the most mysterious things about "it"—that core fire in your gut, that urge to live your life for what matters—is that the experiences that often spark it are the same ones we could just as easily blame for making us feel so weak, depressed, exempt, and inadequate.

My dad, for example, grew up in an abusive home, a family system that just floated on its back in alcoholism, almost as if it was a tradition of the clan. He was raised in the era of the five-mile walk to school (uphill both ways). Except some of those hardscrabble recollections are actually true. Like living in upstate New York, no more than thirty miles from the Canadian border, he would sometimes—as an eight-, nine-, ten-year-old kid—work as many as five hours through the afternoon shoveling snow from driveways in frigid temperatures just to bring home a few dollars, anything to help his struggling family. But his mom—as often as not, when she thought he wasn't looking—would give most of the money to one of his brothers so they could go out and buy booze with it.

Pitiful. Mean.

He also was a pretty good athlete. I guess shoveling snow is every bit as good a workout (or better) as you get at those fancy training gyms with all their huge banks of treadmills, TVs, and kettlebells. He played some basketball in his time, even a little semipro baseball. But his dad—my grandfather—only saw him play in person *once* in all his years of growing up. And even that time he just slipped in, slipped out, and left unnoticed. My dad didn't even know he was there. Despite all the times my father had gone down to the bar, hoisted his dad up on a child-sized shoulder, and toted him back home in that plastered condition, he could never count on him to be there for him. Even for the little things. Hardly at all.

The point I'm making is this: childhood memories like that can kill you. Betrayal, neglect, a complete lack of concern or interest, an utter devaluation of your worth as a person. In many ways, in fact, my dad was a Ranch kid, an emotional orphan, his own family even working against him. And based on where he came from, he could've bobbed along in that same rotten stream for the rest of his life without anybody ever being shocked by it. That's what most everybody else did.

But, no.

He went another way with it instead.

He poured himself into other people. I grew up watching a man who, despite the fact that money was always pretty tight for us, would often pull out ten dollars he couldn't afford from his pocket to give to somebody who was struggling and needed help.

He poured himself into me. I went on to play a lot of sports, which meant going anywhere my teams' schedules took us, all through high school, including college football games everywhere from Tuscaloosa to Texas, from New Orleans to Los Angeles, and tons of places in between. But my dad, rest his soul, only missed being there for *two* of those games throughout my whole playing career—one because of a death in the family, the other to go be with an ill sister or brother.

And what's more, he never poured himself a single drink.
Ever. At eighty-five years old, he and I were riding around in the
truck one day, just talking, reminiscing. And he told me, during the course of conversation, that he had never let one drop of
alcohol cross his lips. "I saw what it did and what it can do, son.
I didn't want my family to have to live with that."

That's "it" in my book.

That's turning the tables on some terrible stuff and not
repeating history.

And it's a big part of what turned me into the person I am
today. What I saw in him was a pattern of belief and action that
consistently lined up with each other. Even with every reason in
the world for not doing it, he just determined in his heart to go
out and get it. And the ripple effect has carried "it" down into
my own life and calling.

Another significant memory for me happened when I was
five years old. Coach Bryant was always fond of telling us how
in every ball game there are sure to be four or five plays that
will directly impact the outcome and how in life it's much the
same. Look back through your own experience and see if that
isn't true. See if you can't locate four or five landmark occasions
that stand out among all the hundred thousand others, moments
that have proven to be pivotal in shaping who you are. A word
spoken. A scene witnessed. A trust broken. A challenge faced.
How did you handle it? What did you do with it? What have you
done with it since?

Critical.

The night before our family was set to attend a funeral
in a nearby community, my sister Lisa and I were fussing at
home over which song to play on the record player. I wanted
to hear "Davy Crockett" or something, and she was crying
about wanting to play "The Yellow Rose of Texas," as I recall.
A typical childhood sibling battle. And as in most typical dis-
agreements involving four- and five-year-olds, we couldn't land

on a workable solution without kicking ourselves up into a big argument. Before long my dad was in there, working to separate us, giving both of us the spanking and tongue-lashing we well deserved.

Crisis averted, we were still up to no good the following day in the graveyard. Oblivious to the solemnity of the moment, we decided to conquer our boredom by straddling two of the parallel tombstones in that part of the cemetery and pretending to be horse racing against each other. At one point, hopping off, I ran up toward the next one in the row, climbed aboard, and hollered back over my shoulder to Lisa, "I'm *win*-ning! I'm *win*-ning!"

That's when I heard it. A heavy thud, a sickening, choking gasp. Then I turned to see the three-hundred-pound tombstone she'd been sitting on now crushing my little sister.

She would not survive. Two ribs had punctured her heart; another two, her lungs—quickly enough that even when my dad, surging with desperate adrenaline, had heaved the leaden weight of that slab single-handedly off and away from Lisa's body, she was still chewing her gum, despite being completely unconscious, almost instantly dead.

My mom, collapsing in the hospital floor later when the doctor came out and wearily shook his head, was basically a zombie for the next three months. I never saw her cry any tears that whole time. Just hurt. Numb. Gone.

My dad, who I don't think ever got over torturing himself for letting go of Lisa's hand that day so she could come play with me or for the fact that his last real interaction with her had been scolding her and spanking her and sending her off to bed the night before, went almost totally gray-headed in six weeks.

And me, just five years old, I was confused by it all, naturally. Traumatized. Stunned by this sudden disruption to our fun, happy, family dynamic.

But for everything that was taken away from me and from us in that horrible tragedy, I look back now and can see something important I gleaned from what I went through. Losing her in that way gave me an emotional strength and toughness that, I believe, propelled me in the direction my future would ultimately take.

I'm not saying, of course, that I'm glad my sister was killed or that God took her life partly in order to impact hundreds of other lives through her brother. Not at all. But on many days when I've sat there looking into the eyes of a little girl who's been hurt by her daddy—sexually abused, perhaps, from the age of three on— I've been able to take care of what that child needs without falling to pieces in front of her, without being overcome by emotion in the face of her suffering, no matter how torn up I may feel inside.

At times I've sat there listening to the infuriating ramblings of a man I'm *almost sure* has done horrible things to his son or daughter, and yet—despite the anger that's clawing my fingernails into my pants leg—I'm able to stay focused on that little boy or girl. Inside, I may be tapping the trigger, itching to rip the guy's throat out. Don't think it hasn't crossed my mind more than once. But that won't do anything at that moment to make the situation better. Getting this child to safety will.

You've got to be emotionally in control to do that.

And one of the ways God has allowed me to develop whatever "it" does to keep me on a calm enough, even enough keel so that I can help these hundreds of kids who've come through our doors, I believe it sprouted and grew from a gnarly, bitter root the day my sister lost her life under a full sun in an Alabama graveyard. The emotional muscle that's given me the stability to do what I do, and to be who I am, for the past forty years, is largely the result of a circumstance that could've gone a whole lot of other bad directions.

I'm just saying that if you're feeling limited by your past, or feeling like you're not up to the task of anything better than average, and yet always feeling as though you're missing something more, which keeps you feeling discouraged and dissatisfied . . .

you can rise above anything you've come from. You can turn it into something good. If I've learned anything from my own life, as well as from the lives of all these kids we've raised, it's that nothing in your past has the power within itself to negatively determine your future. There's nothing that can't be overcome and diverted into blessing.

And the day you start living and thinking that way, that's the day "it" starts growing out all over you.

What You Don't Know

The origins of Big Oak Ranch go back to a twelve-hundred-square-foot farmhouse, deep in the woods, back there with nothing but a couple of little fishing lakes, armies of mosquitoes, and two chicken houses I don't think even chickens would've wanted to live in.

But come to think of it, those first five boys and I probably didn't have any business living in the house we stayed in either. The walls were lined with thin, cottonseed insulation, worked around cloth-wrapped electrical wiring. It was a firetrap if nothing else. But I didn't know any better, and—young and stupid—I never really stopped to think about it.

In fact, I'll tell you just how stupid I was. A guy came out to the little high school one day where I was helping as an assistant football coach, wanting to talk to me and ask some questions. Six months before, I'd been playing for the University of Alabama, number one in the country, in front of eighty-five thousand people at the Sugar Bowl against number three Notre Dame. Turned out to be one of those "games of the century"—a 25.3 Nielsen rating, which (I think) meant that one-fourth of the nation was tuned in from somewhere in America on television that New Year's Eve night.

On this day, however, I was roaming the spotty practice field of a little AA football school in the rural South, when this short, nasally voiced man approached and asked if I was John Croyle.

"Yes, sir, I am. How you doing?"

"Mr. Croyle," he said, "we understand you have children around your home, that these children are living with you."

"That's right."

"Well, sir, do you have a license?"

"A license? Sure, I've got a license," at which point I reached into my back pocket, pulled out my wallet, and handed him my driver's license.

Stupid.

I honestly didn't know I needed government paperwork and permission to do what I was doing.

So we took care of that, of course. But nothing could make up for how ill prepared I was, thinking I could raise five street-smart boys out there in the rugged countryside and expect anything good to come of it. I'm talking about teenage bruisers, some of whom had been living in boxcars and Volkswagen Beetles. One's father had committed suicide; his mom was in a mental institution. One had been unjustly accused of arson. But still, probably not the best mix for that tinderbox of a house I was telling you about.

I tell our kids today sometimes, "Y'all wouldn't have lasted two minutes with that original bunch. They were *rough,* I'm telling you. They would've beat your brains in and eaten you up for dinner." If I'm joking, it's not by much.

And even by the time Tee and I had gotten married, even by the time we'd hired a few staff and established some semblance of an organization, it was a wonder how on some days we were able to get the mail in. I mean, it was just *sad* how ignorant I was of what all this work entailed.

A fellow came by, for instance, and ended up talking me into building an A-frame structure there on the property, persuading me that it would be a good plan for the way our ministry was expanding and how our number of boys was growing. But a little more than a year after we put it up, we had to just tear it down and rebuild. Wasn't working at all.

I didn't have a clue on how to do this ranch. I just knew I had to do it.

But I don't ever remember hearing or reading in the Bible—unless I missed church on that Sunday—that God can't use our ignorance. And if I *had* read it, I don't know if I'd believe it because I've seen it happen over and over again, as much ignorance as I've given Him to work with. When almost every high school graduate, on the night we confer their diplomas on them, stands up in the ceremony and says, "I just want to thank Mr. John and Mrs. Tee for building the Ranch and giving me a home," that's not a testament to *us*. It's testament to God who does incredible things with willing yet ignorant people.

Ignorance is not our problem. Ignorance doesn't keep us from having "it."

But *arrogance*, now—

That's the thing that'll squash "it" down to nothing. When arrogance becomes *who you are*, you're not going to like where it takes you.

And I do know I've heard *that* in the Bible.

"The LORD hates six things; in fact, seven are detestable to Him"—and the first one on the list is: "arrogant eyes" (Prov. 6:16–17). "I hate arrogant pride," His Word says (Prov. 8:13). "When pride comes, disgrace follows" (Prov. 11:2). "Arrogance leads to nothing but strife" (Prov. 13:10). "Pride comes before destruction, and an arrogant spirit before a fall" (Prov. 16:18).

It's everywhere in Scripture.

And if we're not careful, it'll be everywhere in us.

If you don't know how to do something, if you don't know what to do next, if you don't know how to get out of whatever funk or rut or habit or mind-set has been chaining you down to discontentment and defeat, that's not the heart of your problem, not knowing. Nobody knows everything, no matter what they say. And not knowing doesn't mean you can't learn. If that weren't true, I would've failed at this a long time ago.

But while *ignorance* can be taught, *arrogance* can only be broken. Pulverized. Splintered. Smashed into a thousand pieces, then scrubbed hard to make sure every last speck makes it to the dustpan. Arrogance before a holy God is never a winning play—even the backhanded, passive arrogance that says you don't amount to anything, and therefore you don't see how even somebody as big and powerful as Almighty God can change things for you.

But when we put our arrogance up on the anvil, wanting it to be pounded out of us, we then can become people who are bigger than our backgrounds. We become people who cannot be summarized by the stereotype of where we've come from. Sure, we may still be ignorant in some areas, still needing to learn, even with our best attempts at growing and expanding our intellect. But we'll be smart enough to know we've been created by an enormous God, which—among other things, such as making us feel loved and unique and validated by our Maker—should set us up for being properly humble in His presence, don't you think?

And if we'll follow through on that direction, rather than copping an attitude of arrogance, rather than trying to fool everybody else with how together we are, I believe we put ourselves in position for God to come around each morning and tell us something we all need to hear, something that'll wake up our sleeping hopes for significance quicker than a straight shot of black coffee.

Tag—you're it.

You're getting it.

And when you've got it, there's nothing or nobody who can ever take it away from you.

CHAPTER 2

Focus

You've Got a Job to Do

I don't pretend to be a NASCAR driver. Now the traffic cops who hide behind tree-brush frontage out here on the country roads where we live may beg to differ. But as someone who's actually tried racing some practice laps on an official, regulation speedway, I can assure you—the old taunt about Sprint Cup drivers not being real athletes (the same way NFL linebackers are) is outright bogus. There's nothing easy about stock-car racing, even with nobody else out there rubbing your fenders or running four-wide through the turns with you, fighting you for position.

Like I said, Tee and I had a chance to go to Talladega a few years ago, complete with the privilege of doing ten or twenty trips around the big oval, accompanied by an experienced driver in the passenger seat for protection. *And it was awesome.* All that speed. All that noise. Mashing the pedal and revving that race car up to 175 on the back straightaway—talk about your thrill of a lifetime! Can't quite describe it for you if you've never done it.

But, boy, is it ever easy to feel out of control in that kind of driving environment. The rate of incline in the corners is so extreme—up to thirty-three-degree angles in spots, some of the steepest banking in all of racing—that if you were to go less than seventy mph through there, your car would just slither down sideways onto the apron, like it was falling off a collapsed bridge. So as a driver, you bear down and try holding her steady; you feel the centrifugal force pushing you back into your seat; your car hugs the turn. But everything inside your amateur mind is screaming at you to overcompensate for what you're feeling—whatever it takes to keep from careening into the wall or flying up into the fence mesh—while you're working hard to keep your speed up at the same time.

So as I was pulling out of one of those turns, my guide spoke up and told me to notice something I was doing with the steering wheel. "Every time you make that little twitch, that little correction," he said, "you lose about a tenth of a second."

Hmm, hadn't recognized that. But he was right. The caution I felt in driving that fast on such an unfamiliar terrain was making me want to constantly adjust the wheel position—left-right, left-right—even if just a hair, in order to give myself the comfort of thinking that I was keeping the car safely inside the racing groove. But that slight hand motion, going *this* way, then checking back the *other* way, was costing me speed and precision that in a real race would've meant the difference between competing for the win and running dead last. A few miles per hour is usually all that separates the checkered flag from the bottom finisher.

In fact, when Tee climbed in—not as a driver but just to ride with the guy who'd gone around with *me*—they were able to go 185 in the same car, a full ten mph faster.

Both of us, of course, had driven the same stretch, traveling the same direction, operating under the same conditions. And yet the other man reached the finish line much faster and quicker than I did. Why? Because he held it steady and never wavered.

Because he knew how to *focus*.

One of the real secrets to mastering *who you are* and living it out with drive and purpose is the discipline of staying intently focused on what you're supposed to be doing.

Who You Are, Who You're Not

Hang around as long as I've been here, and you begin to realize—both from your good days and your bad days—just how tiny the difference between success and failure can often be. Sometimes, like out on that track at Talladega, a slight bit of wobble in your focus is all it takes to miss the mark. But if you can lock in, hold your course, trust your instincts and your instruments, you're able to whip through even the toughest bends in the track and still slingshot out on the other end, hitting your stride, maximizing your effort, totally smoking. Feels good.

So one of the things I've tried really hard to master over the years is the ability to stay completely concentrated on what I've set out to do. And of the few traits I see being strong in me— among the many that I don't have—I think the commitment and focus we've strived to maintain at Big Oak Ranch have been truly instrumental to what we've been able to accomplish.

It all starts with knowing who you *are*, knowing who you're *not*, and then being disciplined enough with yourself that you don't weave in and out of your own lane as you're rolling forward.

Think about it. The compassion that drives any of us—you, me, whoever—into wanting to serve and care for others is a fine inspiration for trying to help people. But if you let that same sense of compassion veer you all over the place, letting it be your only driver, taking you outside whatever wise boundaries you've established to serve you as a guide, you'll consistently find yourself being off track. You'll end up diluting and hindering your effectiveness in doing what God's designed you to do because you're foolishly, recklessly trying to do too much. And while it sounds all good and noble to want to follow your heart like that, the flip side is always worth recognizing. You could unwittingly be doing harm instead of good to people by taking time and resources away from the few, all in a rash attempt to be everything for everyone.

See what I mean? You've got to stay on course.

When we take a child into one of our homes, for example, part of the intake process involves determining just how seriously they're hurt and what kind of care they're likely to need in order to put their identity back together. Some of the children who come to us are not torn apart as badly as others, and our houseparents are amply qualified to steer them through their various obstacles. Most of the kids, however, have been anywhere from significantly abused to absolutely devastated, their sense of value and normalcy just shredded. And so we know we'll need to make sure we give them discreet access to the kind of competent, professional counseling that'll help them repackage what's been littered so cruelly and haphazardly all over their hearts.

I'm making this sound a lot simpler than it actually is, of course, but you get the idea. We've got staff and processes in place to help us make sure we give each kid exactly what he or she needs in order to recover and thrive.

That's the goal. That's the focus.

But we've concluded from long history, as well as from a rugged evaluation of what our specific role is supposed to be, that a couple of categories and situations that steer people into our driveway are not the main focus of our mission—meaning we're likely not the best fit for what those children need.

One subset of kid that we've determined is not within our scope of ministry is the *spoiled brat*. Or, to put it more accurately, the selectively blind parent who's *created* the spoiled brat—the mom or dad who comes into my office, practically dragging their child by the ear, and says, "I'm done! I've had it with him!"

"Well, what did he do?"

"I'm just sick of his back talking."

"*Back* talking? Why's he doing that?

The boy jumps in. "I'll tell you why. I heard her tell somebody on the phone the other day, 'I can't stand him. He looks just like my ex. He's just a little version of his dad, and I hate him.' I heard you say it, Mom."

"Oh, I didn't mean that," she says, embarrassed to hear this little detail coming out.

Her son looks away from her and rolls his eyes, mumbling "Yeah, right" under his breath.

"See?" she says, turning back to me. "I've had it with his sass. I'm done! *You* take him."

Well, you know what? I can see where each of them—both the mom *and* the child—could stand for somebody to jerk a knot in their respective tails. In fact, I wouldn't mind doing it myself, to be honest with you. But, listen, I've got kids living here at the Ranch who don't have *anybody*, whose parents would still be pimping them out on the street if we were to send them back home, whose dad's poker buddies used to play each other on Friday nights for the chance of taking the dad's daughter back into the next room—a little, trembling ten-year-old girl— as part of winning the pot. She was the prize. You hear what I'm saying? And I'm supposed to get in the middle of a mom and her son whose only real problem is that they can't keep their idiotic mouths shut?

I don't think so.

Our job, the way we see it, is not to fix parents—parents who don't know what to do with their kids anymore. Our job, like we say in our motto, is to be "a Christian home for children needing a chance." And, as far as I'm concerned, spoiled brats and their parents are able to make their *own* chances if they'll just slow down long enough to understand each other.

We're not turning Big Oak Ranch into a summer camp to try fixing fifteen years of parents' careless inadequacies, the kind that spit out nothing but a trash-talking, entitled teenager. No sir. I'll make room for *any* kids who need what we can offer them. We'll never turn *anyone* away, even if we need to bed them down on the floor or find some other arrangement that'll work for a little while until we can free up the space. But not if they and their parents are too dumb to see what they've got. Not if they're brats.

To do so would only get us off our focus.

Then there's one other broad category which, for right now at least, requires us to partner with other programs who offer something we're not currently set up to do. Part of the challenge involved in performing our kind of ministry is recognizing when we're beyond our capabilities, times when a child is brought to us whose needs are simply out of our league. If we *know* we're not equipped to help this boy or girl, if we *know* he or she needs things from us that we cannot capably provide, we're not only keeping that kid from getting the right kind of immediate, acute, emergency care they require, but we're setting them up to fail again. It's a lose-lose for everybody.

I'm talking about the grandmother, for example, who asked if I'd be willing—begged me, actually, practically down on her knees—to take custody of her two grandsons, ages ten and twelve.

"What seems to be the problem?" I asked.

"Well, we've got to go to court tomorrow."

"Oh, really? What happened?"

"I just need you to take my grandchildren for me, Mr. Croyle."

[long breath] "Ma'am, I'm trying to help you, but you're going to need to tell me what the issues are."

"It's just that we've got to be in court tomorrow at ten. And I need to know right now what you can do for them. Please? Will you take them? Please?"

We went round and round like this for a few minutes longer . . . before the awful truth finally came out.

Her grandsons had murdered their parents.

Theirs was one of those homes, apparently, where the mom and dad had been particularly strict. And as happens in a small percentage of cases, the family dynamics had grown toxic enough until somebody snapped and began seriously considering mortal violence as a way to deal with their problems.

The older son had dragged his little brother out of bed one night, telling him he needed help with something. The ten-year-old later testified on the witness stand that he remembered only two things from the rest of that night's events: the shrieks of his mother, yelling to her sons to come get the killer off of them (not realizing in the dark that her own boy was the one doing it), and the plunging, slicing sound of the knife, cutting into and out of his parents' bodies, over and over.

"They're being sentenced in the morning," the woman in front of me finally admitted. "And the judge says if *you'd* take them, Mr. Croyle, he'd let you have them."

I'm asking you—do you think you'd feel any compassion for a poor grandma in that situation, not wanting her grandsons to be thrown in jail if there was any chance, as the judge had allegedly said, that they could do their time at a nice place like this? Think you could walk her, crying, sobbing, out the door, and say, "Ma'am, we just can't help you"?

But it was the right call to make.

Because that's not who we are.

Accepting kids who are clearly out of our league would dilute and threaten what we're doing for the hundred or so others who trust us to keep them safe from what life has done to them. It's not being uncompassionate to think that way; it's being uncompromising.

It's having *focus*.

Great Moments in Focus

Focus is what Coach Bryant brought to our teams at Alabama. He would say to guys who were just entering the program, at the first team meeting: "Don't worry about proving to us how good of a football player you are. Don't come out here trying to show us what you've got. Just join us, and let's go win a national championship."

It's no lie to say, from what I experienced in real life as an Alabama football player, we moved from scrimmage play to scrimmage play, from practice drill to practice drill, with one single goal in mind at all times: winning the national championship. It's what drove us to get better. It's what drove us out of our beds every morning, past the alarm clock to the weight room, past the soreness, fatigue, and injuries. And it's why we drove most all our opponents into the ground—anyone who dared to stand in our way. It's why we lost only one regular season game in three years.

That's focus.

It's what American soldiers saw in General Patton, like in that meeting depicted in the George C. Scott movie, the scene where the Allied leaders were strategizing on how to support the 101st Airborne division, who was pinned down at Bastogne. Holding that key position against the enemy was imperative. Without it they might lose the war. But with it they might break up the entire German offensive.

Patton said, "I can attack with three divisions in forty-eight hours," referring to his Third Army, the troops under his command.

"Impossible, George. That's over a hundred miles." Not only were his men already engaged in an active mission at their current coordinates, but the harsh, impassable weather made overland travel slow and treacherous—winter, cold, snow. "You can't cart them off a hundred miles in two days and then expect them to attack without rest."

"Yes, I can."

"Be reasonable. How?"

"They'll do it because I ask them."

And they did.

That's focus.

It's what Jethro, the father-in-law of Moses, inspired in him as the great leader of Israel. The older man, passing through, was impressed by what Moses and his God had been able to accomplish. But he was also puzzled at why his son-in-law was filling his whole day, from morning till night, trying to handle the various conflicts and disputes of all the people, all by himself. "What you're doing is not good," Jethro told him. "You will certainly wear out both yourself and these people who are with you, because the task is too heavy for you. You can't do it alone" (Exod. 18:17–18).

So he advised Moses to delegate some of his duties to other men he could trust, then empower those people to determine whenever an issue arose that was major enough to justify Moses' time and help. That way he could be fresh and freed up to hear from God and maintain his boldness and vision. By delegating he could become a much stronger leader.

That's focus.

And it's what Jesus, of course, exemplified perfectly as He followed His mission to the cross. Imagine the distractions that played in His human mind—not only the justified fears of

His upcoming torture and punishment but also the hundreds of people still blind, lame, and hurting all around Him whose deliverance from their diseases could've brought so much comfort and joy to His own heart—perhaps even a change of mind to this murderous mood that was swirling about the city and countryside.

But He knew He was called to something even bigger. The healing He was prepared to bring would go deeper and last longer than any roadside miracle. So He kept His eyes on the goal. He did exactly what He needed to do each day. He stayed focused.

His friends, the central core of His disciples, didn't have *any* focus. On the night when Jesus was sweating drops of blood in the garden, they were nodding off to sleep nearby, not able to stay awake even one hour to pray for Him and offer their support. But as Isaiah had prophesied years before, most likely referring to Jesus the Messiah, "I have set My face like flint, and I know I will not be put to shame" (Isa. 50:7).

That's focus.

And if we expect to see our endeavors take shape and take flight, that's what we all need. Focus is foundational in staying true to *who you are.*

Go back to that experience I was describing on the racetrack at Talladega—those small movements I was making with the steering wheel, enough that they were slowing down my speed and efficiency through the turns. Think of each pull to the right or the left as a sin—a glance, a look, an attitude, a word, a compromise, a fit of anger, a harbored resentment. It may just be brief. Or it may be ingrained and ongoing. But whatever it is, it's stealing your focus. And it's causing you to lose, more often than you win.

That's why the Bible doesn't flinch in telling us to lock down our compass settings and snap a beeline for true north. "Let your eyes look forward; fix your gaze straight ahead" (Prov. 4:25).

"Don't let your heart turn aside" to anything (Prov. 7:25). Instead, "strengthen your tired hands and weakened knees, and make straight paths for your feet, so that what is lame may not be dislocated but healed instead" (Heb. 12:12–13).

Get the hitch out of your steering wheel, in other words.

Know where you're going and what it takes to get there.

And develop an instant radar alert for anything that lures you away from the dead-ahead direction you intend to go.

Stay focused.

Detractors and Distractions

As many success stories as we've seen come to life on our campus here and as much of a feel-good story as Big Oak Ranch has become for a lot of people who pass by or hear about us or read an interview in some magazine somewhere, we also get our fair share of critics—folks who look to find fault in what we're doing.

Questioning our focus.

"They only take perfect kids," I've heard people say. "That's why they're all so polite and respectful—yes sir, no sir."

Well, that's just not true. Every kid who has ever called Big Oak Ranch their home is one or more of the following: (1) orphaned, (2) abused, (3) neglected, (4) abandoned, and/or (5) homeless. Does that sound "perfect" to you? But God in His grace—not to mention a shot in the arm of strong work ethic, discipline, personal responsibility, and a whole lot of trust-building and love—has turned hundreds of fractured young boys and girls into people who know how to handle themselves—how to look you in the eye and smile, say "thank you" and "please," and be prepared to enter the world with a good sense of rightful authority and self-esteem.

We can't let people who don't understand us bog us down or discourage us.

Other critics, as I've mentioned, have taken issue with some of our policies on how we determine which kids we can help and which ones we can't. "Well, you didn't take one of *my* children. You said she was 'out of your league.' But you took two others that same week, I heard. What's up with that?"

I tell people all the time, "We're cardio surgeons, not neurosurgeons." We're thankful for programs that can zero in on the severely traumatized kids whose situations call for intensive, institutional, almost one-to-one care—children who wouldn't be able to function and share with others well in a home environment with seven other siblings in the house. But for forty years, we've tried to stay true to our calling of mending broken hearts. And we've seen it beat out a steady rhythm of blessing and change in hundreds of children's lives. I'm not apologizing for that.

Or there's the stance we've taken, which I told you about, where we don't expend energy on parents who need help with their wayward, rebellious, spoiled kids. I've even needed to let certain staff members go when we couldn't see eye to eye on this position. But I've learned through the years that one of the measurements of a leader is knowing when it's appropriate to fire an employee—not because you're slinging a hatchet and throwing your weight around but because you can't afford for your team to lose its focus.

A man came to see me not too long ago, begging me to help his sixteen-year-old daughter. He was a big-time executive, way up the food chain in his particular field. Worked for a huge company, had a high-level position. And his child, quite frankly, had been acting like an idiot. "Would y'all be willing to take her for a little while and fix her?" he asked.

Like I said—and like you can imagine—it's hard to turn a child away. And on another level it's hard to know that by saying no to a millionaire, who otherwise would be kindly disposed toward your nonprofit ministry, you're probably costing yourself a sizable annual contribution.

But I knew what I needed to do.

Because you can't be what you're not. You've got to be *who you are*. The minute you lose your focus, you're taking yourself down a path that can't help but do more harm than good. For everybody.

As my daughter Reagan (director of our child-care team) so wisely said, when I went to talk with her about it, "How do you think it'd make our girls feel to see this spoiled, rich, prima donna come in here—a girl who's *got* a home—just to hang out for a little while in the only home our children have? How *demeaning* that would be to our kids."

Yes, how demeaning.

Some things can feel right when they're actually wrong. But in the end nothing feels much worse than knowing your lack of focus has caused you to fail.

Any ballplayer will tell you, you can't swing for the fences on every at-bat. Sometimes, to stay focused, you've got to pick your spots. Play to your strengths. Follow the game plan. In our case, at least, I don't want to do anything that keeps our kids from being encouraged every time they connect on a solid single or double, every time they make good choices, laying down bunts for one another, rallying from behind. I want them to be proud to see themselves just staying in the base paths, making it safely from station to station after so many years of being forced to swing at hard fastballs with one hand tied behind their backs.

Does everybody understand that? No.

Do I care what they think? Not really.

Being focused is sure to attract detractors just as quickly as it attracts distractions. But you can't let that throw you. You can't let others define the road for you that God Himself has called you to travel.

So let 'em talk. You can't stop them from doing that. Let confusion or compromise tempt you. It can only pull you as far off course as you allow it. And when somebody comes along, trying to force you into being somebody you're not, I hope you'll simply smile, say "excuse me," step directly through the perceived obstacle, and go right on your way.

Becoming a Natural

If you were to drive up on the site of a traffic accident and notice to your shocked surprise that one of the damaged vehicles looked awfully familiar—"dear God, that's my daughter's car!"—you'd raise your head up, pull quickly over, throw the transmission into park, and run directly toward the scene.

As your brain adjusts to what you're seeing and feeling, you hear the distinctive sound of your daughter's voice pierce through the confusion, screaming in pain. Maybe her legs are pinned under the dashboard. Maybe she's smashed her head against the windshield. You don't know. But as you navigate around the other cars, hustling toward the sound of her despair, you catch sight of a drunken man in your peripheral vision, reeling around on the slick pavement, slurring through loud, husky words. "An-y-bod-y huurrt?" he says.

Part of your thought process at that moment—all things being equal—would be to go ram that so-and-so flat across the trunk of his car, maybe shove him over a guardrail and off into the drainage ditch, not caring what he hit on his way down.

But that's not what you do. Because, yes, you *hear* him. You're *aware* of him. His presence by the roadside helps you begin to gather information about what's happened. But your gut makes you run straight toward your daughter. She's all you care about. Her help and safety are the only things that interest you in that moment.

She's your focus.

That's because you'd already determined, before a situation like this could even arise to test you, what your main priorities are. Doesn't matter that your impulses are being challenged. Doesn't matter that you're being presented with two or more options for how to deal with the same situation. You know who you are—"I'm a parent." You know what your job is—"I'm here to take care of my daughter." And so you just do it.

Naturally.

Maintaining a sharp focus can sometimes sound fairly complicated. And I admit, it does often mean making tough choices and ticking some people off. But the upshot of it is usually pretty basic and simple. It doesn't require a huge master plan, color coded and long-range, with all kinds of vision statements and wraparound 360-degree analysis. It doesn't mean declaring that every single thing you've been doing so far is dead wrong and needs to be completely blown up if you've got any chance at succeeding.

Don't psych yourself out. Don't make this any harder than it needs to be. Just get a good feel for who you are. Get a good feel for who you're not. And not only will you start to see your future more clearly, but you'll much more naturally start making the kinds of daily decisions that lead you where you want to go.

You'll be focused. And you'll be fine.

CHAPTER 3

Stand

You're in This for Life

I like places that have been here for a while. I like hardware stores where the gray-haired man working the cash register can tell you how to sweat a copper pipe and knows exactly which box, on which aisle, on which shelf, contains the kind of solder and plumbing flux you need for doing it.

I like greasy breakfast joints where the same old four guys have been showing up at 6:30 every weekday morning for twenty some-odd years, talking football and solving the world's problems, washing down their bacon and eggs with a stout cup of coffee in an honest-to-goodness coffee mug.

I like traditions that go back generations, the kind that people can mark time with, remembering how they used to get together as a family at their grandfather's house on some of those special days, at some of those special seasons of the year, back when they were kids.

And so I like being able, at Big Oak Ranch, to carve the words "Established in 1974" right there into the cement—a year that will certainly sound more and more ancient as time goes by, when little boys and girls who need a chance are still finding a home here, long after I'm dead and gone, the same way it's happened for the past four decades.

Yeah, we've been doing this a long time.

And I like that.

We live in a day when, modern technology being what it is, some hotshot with a gimmick can time things right and be able to attract an immediate flash of overnight attention. He'll make the circuit around the TV talk shows, get written up in the newspapers, and think he's suddenly become important just because his phone is ringing.

We also live in a day when the right combination of marketers, advertisers, and publicity dollars can purchase enough airtime and media exposure to basically *buy* a brand image for their product, their performer, or their client's persona. Instant fame is often available to the highest bidder.

But you can't buy heritage. You can't fake history. You can't pretend you've been around for years if you just showed up last month. You can't be "established in 1974" just because you woke up this morning and wanted to be. *Some* things, *some* blessings, only come from staying true to *who you are* and being willing to stick with it for a long time.

What about *you*? Are you in for the long haul?

I'm not bragging about this because I honestly just consider myself extremely blessed, honored, privileged, thankful—humbled, actually—that God somehow barged into my hard ol' head early in life and made it really clear what He wanted me to do. I know it doesn't work like that for everybody, and I'm not saying it *should*. But by the time some special people helped me put a start to the Ranch, way back all those years ago, I didn't have any doubt I'd be doing this for the rest of my life. Maybe I was just too stubborn to think any different, but that's the way I felt about it.

And while, again, I'm not implying that something's wrong with a person who doesn't latch on to the first job they land at twenty-three and ride it all the way into the sunset, I *do* think some of what distinguishes those people who have "it" from those who don't is the courage and farsighted wisdom to see life as a long-term deal.

Long-term commitments.

Long-term relationships.

Long-term promises.

Long-term goals.

Now perhaps, from whatever vantage point you're looking at life today, this line of thinking doesn't feel too encouraging to you. Or doesn't seem to apply. Maybe you're fairly young, for example, and you're not seeing the need for planning so far ahead. You're either happy with how things are going, pretty much, or if not, you're just trying to survive your current circumstances till something better comes along. Not really thinking too far beyond the immediate future right now.

Or perhaps, even though you may not be so young anymore, one of the things that really bugs you about yourself is that you haven't exactly been a symbol of steadiness over the years. It's been more up and down, stop and start, hit and miss. Not those nice, long runs of staying the course. Your days are really busy, I'm sure. You meet yourself coming and going. But as far as having a deep sense of vision, as far as knowing where you're really headed in life, being confident that you're making progress toward your biggest, most important aims and desires—you're just not all that sure. And because of it, you may not be all that pleased at the moment with yourself or with your track record.

But remember what I talked about at first? Remember what the past is for? It's for being honest and up front about who you've *been*. It's for taking good stock of what's happened to you and how you've handled it, of what you've done and what you've learned from it. But it's not for defining the person you're fatally destined to be like forever. Sure, it's for being man or woman enough, in recognizing your mistakes and weaknesses, not to gloss over a single one of them or to hide behind excuses for why you've been less than your best in any number of different areas, like all of us have. But by looking back and looking around from a healthy point of view, you can see what's gotten you here to this point. And you can see where you need to go.

Which means the long haul is still out there in front of you.

You haven't missed it.

It hasn't passed you by.

In fact, you're now at the best place in the world to go grab hold of it. To plant both feet firmly in the middle of it. And to refuse to turn loose of it. To stay in this thing for life. From now on.

That's the part that really matters—the "from now on" part.

Because if you're courageous enough to start fresh, renewing a long-term, long-haul quality to your life, you'll begin to embody or improve upon some valuable traits that will mean more to you than all the money you could make and all the accomplishments you could accumulate.

Let's talk about a few of those.

Reputation

My dad always said, "If you're going to do something, don't just—" (let's see, how can I say this in a Christian book) ". . . don't just do it halfway."

The word he used had a little more bite to it, but I think the term *halfway* gets the general point across.

He meant not doing a shoddy job on stuff. Not bothering to build something or fix something or work on something if you don't intend to make it last. I mean, what's the use? Why not go ahead and just take the time now to do it the way it's supposed to be done instead of having to come back later and do it all over? You know? *That* kind of thing.

String enough of that mind-set together, stretch it out consistently into the future, and what you end up creating as you go along is a *reputation* for doing things well. No half measures. No coasting. No saving it up for your second wind. No shortcuts.

I heard Richard Petty (legendary stock car driver and racing team owner) say one time as I was giving him a tour of the Ranch—"Dang, this is a children's home?" I guess he was expecting to see military-style dormitories, some kind of industrial-grade barracks, with twenty-five, thirty boys shoehorned inside a tin-roofed structure, and a priest in a clerical collar sitting at the end of the hall under a bare light bulb or something. What he saw instead were all-brick, two-story homes, on tree-lined streets, with a handful of cars parked in the driveway and the family hanging out together in the backyard—a scene not enormously different from how things might look on a summer afternoon in most every other neighborhood around.

That's because we're committed to giving our kids a stable, warm, accepting place to live and belong—a well-built house with tasteful landscaping and all the common comforts of home—the way *you'd* want to live, growing up. Normal. Secure. Why shouldn't *they*? Just because they've been harmed at early ages by circumstances beyond their control doesn't mean they need to be institutionalized, branded, treated like an inmate or a case number. They don't need to live in something we tossed up in two weeks that just barely came in under codes. No, we want them in nice bed linens and clean outfits, in a room with a twelve-pane storm window, a ceiling fan, and a nice breeze coming through in the springtime.

And the reason we've done it this way, in large part, is because of that piece of advice from my dad that still rings in my ears just about every day: "Don't do it h—" (whoop, almost said it again)—"Don't do it halfway."

Do it like you mean it.

Do it so it stands up.

Because then people will know, when they're dealing with you, that you're the kind of person who goes all in. When you're on the job, they know you'll be giving it everything you've got. You're not someone who's just trying to make it through the day. The way you see it, you're making *investments* out of today— with everything you do and everything you touch. That's why your work is so sturdy, thorough, high quality, long lasting. And those who interact with you—whether it's your family, a customer, a supervisor, a neighbor—can always count on the fact that the effort you're giving isn't just a one-off, minimum-effort, halfway undertaking. Instead, it's based on and inspired by a long-term commitment you've made, a promise to always drive yourself to excellence and service.

Now that's not a reputation anybody else can give you. They don't hand those out on the street corner or slide them under your wiper blades at the grocery store. Reputation is something you earn over time . . . and then keep building with every new opportunity to do your best.

It's a lifetime thing. A long-haul thing.

Trustworthiness

One of the main promises we make to our children here at the Ranch, you may remember, is "I will never lie to you." And the reason this promise strikes them so powerfully, each time we say it, is because people have been lying to these kids their whole lives. The idea that somebody would actually, finally be truthful with them—even if the truth might hurt sometimes—just wraps around their bodies like a warm blanket. You can see it. Feel it.

So I guard that commitment with my life. And now that my son Brodie is more often the one who officially makes that promise to our new kids—(I'll tell you more about Brodie's role later)—I see in him a man who guards this sacred charge just as tenaciously as I do.

During his initial meeting with a child, when Brodie is formalizing for them what their future is going to be like here with us, he'll turn to the director of the girls' ranch, for example, (if it's a girl) and say, "Jonathan, how long have you been working here?"

"Five years."

"And what would happen to you if you ever lied to one of our girls?"

"I'd be fired. On the spot. I'd be told to start looking for a new job. That day."

Exactly right. And that goes for me too. "Even my *dad*," Brodie tells the kids, "if he ever lies to you—even once—I promise you . . . he's worked his last day at the Ranch." And we mean it.

We take honesty *so* seriously around here.

But as you know, it wouldn't take more than one breach in that commitment, and then all our words and all our promises wouldn't be worth the breath they're spoken with. Wouldn't mean anything anymore. Trustworthiness must be built up over a lifetime. And it can only be *rebuilt* by showing a steady pattern of trustworthiness over a consistent length of months and years—a longer time than you'd want, probably, but not any longer than it takes.

If that's where life is finding you right now—with your trustworthiness in question—there's only one thing for you to do. Be willing to be held accountable to this promise: from now until the day you die, nothing is ever coming out of your mouth again that's not the absolute truth.

Nothing.

One of our older girls asked me, not long ago, "What are you afraid of, Mr. John? Anything?" We were in a van, a bunch of us. I was driving. She was sitting behind me. Several of us were just talking.

"I'm not afraid of any *person*," I said, "even though I'm sure a lot of guys could whip me pretty good. And pretty easy. I'm not as young as I used to be, you know. But—"

I thought for a second. "I guess I *am* afraid of one thing."

"What's that?" she asked.

"I'm afraid of ever doing anything that could possibly hurt you."

That scares me to death.

And one of the ways I could hurt her the worst, I believe— or any of the others—would be by ever failing to deliver on something that I'd told them I would do.

So I'd like to issue this same fearful warning to you. When it comes to some of those daily decisions in your life where you're faced with a choice—"Do I tell the truth, or do I duck around it? Should I do what I said, or just let it go?"—listen up: don't even stop for one second to try mulling over your options. Because if you ever choose to be less than forthcoming about what you've done or haven't done, if you ever decide to make a promise you don't really intend to keep, if you ever think you're protecting yourself by not answering somebody's question in a direct, honest manner, be sure of this: you will end up hurting somebody before it's all over. Could be your wife, your husband. Could be one of your kids. Could be your mom or dad, or somebody else you claim to care a lot about—somebody you'd die if you saw them looking back at you one day, saying to you, "I'm sorry, I just don't believe you. I can't trust you anymore."

Being known as a man or woman of your word—and being sure in your heart that you truly are—is one of the greatest treasures you'll ever own. And the only way to get it is to commit your whole life to it.

Trust me on this one.

Loyalty

I've noticed over the years, I've been able to get a lot of people to come work with us who model the five absolutes we expect of everybody who joins our team: (1) a love for the Lord, (2) a love for children, (3) a teachable heart, (4) a willing spirit, and (5) a loyalty to our leadership and to the Ranch. We've seen some amazing individuals pass through our lives as a result, men and women who've significantly impacted a lot of children and futures along the way.

But almost without fail, if any one of these five qualities I've just mentioned is liable to show signs of cracking, *loyalty* will be the first to go. That's where you'll notice it the quickest. As soon as a person stops believing in where we're going and what we're trying to do—as soon as they don't share our focus and vision anymore—their days are probably numbered as far as how effective they can be at the job they've been tasked with performing.

When loyalty drops off, a lot of other problems are usually right behind.

Simply stated, *loyalty* is another one of those long-haul mentalities that puts you in position for so many good things to happen in your life: meaningful work, fulfilling relationships, a vibrant reality to your faith, a shoulder-to-shoulder unity with others. Good stuff. *Really* good stuff. I'm not saying, of course, that anybody who doesn't believe wholeheartedly in our mission or methods at Big Oak Ranch is a horrible person. Nor am I saying that anybody who doesn't agree with me on every point is sure to be on the wrong side of every argument. (I'm hardly the fount of all wisdom.) But each of us needs to know where our loyalties lie. And once we've decided on them, once we've committed to them, those loyalties need to be strong enough so that no puny, piddling, hissy fit can ever make us throw our hands up and turn against our family, our friends, our coworkers, our authorities, or anybody to whom we've pledged our loyalty, just because they're not making us happy at the moment.

True loyalty isn't that fickle.

And that's why it can really only be proven across the course of a lifetime. That's how you gauge the might and measure of a person's loyalty. But once established and given momentum, once tested and shown to be solid, it creates bonds with others that hold us together no matter what's conspiring against us to pull us apart.

I could tell you right now the names of people on our staff who I know wouldn't fail me under any circumstances. Even if the economy blew up, even if everything went south, even if our only option was to shut off power to the whole shebang and sit down together in one room to pray for a miracle, I know already—from the dedication I've seen on display in certain individuals over the years—which ones would tell me: "I'm here. Let's go. I'll do this job for free. I'll sleep on the gym floor if I need to. Whatever it takes to care for our kids."

That's loyalty.

And it only grows with time.

Persistence

Bobby Allison is a sports Hall of Famer, member of a great racing family, who's graciously helped bring awareness to what we're doing with our kids. Every time I've asked him for anything, he has always been so willing to help out.

He won dozens of races between the mid-1960s and late '80s, competing in the old Winston Cup series, as well as a couple of runs at the Indy 500. He still holds the record for being the oldest driver ever to win at Daytona, pulling off the victory in the 1988 season-opening race at the shifty age of fifty. (How 'bout that?) So when given the chance to meet him for the first time, when we hosted him here at the Ranch, I could tell he was a special breed from the rough-and-tumble heyday of hard-core motor sports.

But I wondered, "What made him so successful?"—which is what I asked the person who'd set this whole thing up for us, as we were standing off to the side together.

Here's what the guy answered me: "Did you notice how he's limping?"

"Yeah," I said.

"You know why he does?"

"Uh-uh, no."

"Because he's got a hole the size of a fifty-cent piece burned into the bottom of his foot . . . from where he wasn't willing to let up off the gas pedal."

The man explained to me that in the Bobby Allison era of racing, gas pedals weren't made out of the same sort of heat-reducing material that comes standard on today's models. The accelerator on a stock car, circa 1970, basically radiated like an iron skillet on the stovetop, conveying heat from the engine and underbelly of the chassis right up through the floorboard. And so whenever he was pressing in on a close finish at some of those hundreds of races he ran, he was also pressing down hard on hundreds of degrees Fahrenheit—and he wouldn't pull off—even if that hot metal was burning layers of flesh right from the ball of his right foot.

Talk about guts. Talk about drive.

Talk about *persistence*.

It's like a story I read recently of a second lieutenant in the Marines during the Vietnam War—a guy named John Bobo, twenty-four years old—who was holding a hill with his outfit against the North Vietnamese. A mortar round, fired from the thick elephant grass in front of them, shot off most of his right leg, just below the knee. He was down. But instead of allowing himself to be helped to safety, and instead of surrendering his firearm, he jammed the stump of his severed leg into the dirt, in an attempt to staunch the bleeding, and kept on firing against the enemy—till a final shot took his life.

Man, that's toughness.

That's *persistence*.

When you start thinking about what you want to be known for—what you want your life to communicate when people take in your whole body of work and experience—

Persistence.

Nobody who's got "it" doesn't have *that*.

There's no residual joy or satisfaction in choosing the safe way, in running for cover, in hanging back with the pack, in sitting out the battle. If you want to start feeling better about *who you are* and who you want to be, start being willing to go to the mat for those things that really matter. Don't just turn in a good performance every now and then. Resolve to grind out an everyday life of character, alertness, endurance . . .

Persistence.

Streaming Reality

Probably the greatest thing that starts coming together, when you truly begin living with a long-run perspective, is just the freedom to be yourself. A lot of people, pretending to be a person they're not, are always in that mode of trying to impress everybody. To fool everybody. But the only person in that scenario that we usually end up fooling is ourselves, stupidly thinking we can always keep the act going and thinking people are buying it.

They're not.

Or at least not for long.

I guess I've been particularly prevented from even entertaining this option because what you find out from being around eight- and eleven- and fifteen-year-olds all the time is that you can't pull the wool over their eyes. Kids, it seems, more than most people, can see through a phony in no time flat. They may not come right out and say it, they may not know exactly how to express it, but you can see it in their demeanor and body language, if you're looking for it, that they're *on* to you. Especially the ones here at the Ranch. They've seen enough fakes and frauds in their lives, they're self-taught not to take people immediately at face value.

But when you're steadily building up a lifetime of stuff like we've been talking about—reputation, trustworthiness, loyalty, persistence—then you don't feel the need to cover up much and try keeping it inside. Whether everybody understands you or not, whether everybody agrees with you or not, you develop a comfort level with *who you are* that just naturally comes out as authenticity, as genuineness.

And you know what? That's just the only way to live.

Doesn't mean we're perfect. I'm sure not. Or anywhere close to it. But only a shortsighted man or woman goes out into each day hoping to tap dance well enough so that people won't notice the true shallowness of their commitment or the lack of thought they've put into where they're going.

To me—what *I've* seen—is that a stream of blessing always runs through life, coming down from God's grace and glory, flowing right past your door. Inside the rush of that rippling stream are all kinds of opportunities and life adventures. Helpful connections with people. Answered prayers. Unexpected wisdom and foresight. The power to carry you over the rocks and rapids of difficulty, helping you navigate the hard runs with a steady hand and a joyful, contented faith.

It's everything you want. Even things you didn't *know* you wanted or needed, but God, in His mercy and love and the desire for His name to be honored through the work you do and the life you live, sends that stream in your direction, offering you the total package of His presence, protection, and provision.

But you don't get to experience the full force of that stream merely by dipping your toe into it, trying not to get wet. It's not a wading stream; it's a riding stream. You jump in, you shove away from the bank, you brace your feet into the hold, your biceps against the oars . . . and you take off.

For good.

For life.

And because God is the source of that stream and the captain of your vessel, you can be sure it'll take you to places that can only be explained by the extent of His goodness and the unlimited nature of His power.

On some days, of course, the long haul can feel longer than others. Bailing out and backing off can sometimes seem like the only alternative that makes any sense or appears safe. But the longest stretches of all, in reality, are those times when you've pulled it in, pulled into yourself, and looked up to see just how far you've drifted from that stream of blessing again.

I know staying committed to your path—to your promises, to your God, to your family, your hopes, your dreams and responsibilities—is rarely easy to maintain. But a stream of His blessing is waiting on you if you'll just go ahead and leap off the side and dive in headfirst.

The best life on earth—for you—can be yours. *Your* life.

But only if you decide to really live it.

From here on.

CHAPTER 4

Soar

You're Not Settling for Less

My goal starting out was to build the best children's home in America. Didn't know exactly what that looked like. Definitely didn't know how much work it would turn out to be or what some of those long, countless hours would come to entail. At the same time I didn't know—couldn't know—the enormous blessings that would pour into my life and my family's life as we kept hacking away at this thing. Nor did I know, to be honest with you, if we'd ever be able to keep it going for this long.

And you know what else? After forty years I *still* don't know what all God has in store for this place and these kids. And for their kids.

But that's OK. Because working to be the best is all I've ever needed to know.

It's all *any* of us needs to know.

Make it much more complicated than that, and here's what happens to us: we end up measuring success by all the wrong scoring systems. We base it on where we started from, then figure we can never catch up with everybody else. Or we base it on what success means to the majority of our friends and to other people our age that we're trying to outperform. Or we base it on rigid goals we've set for ourselves that continually keep success dangling out there in front of us but never right here where we can see it and feel it and experience it and, I don't know, maybe enjoy it a little? Savor it along the way?

The quest for success—when misinterpreted—has a way of spoiling everything. It becomes something maddeningly unattainable. It's like a dark shelf of clouds, heavy, looming, forming up behind you on what started out to be a nice, sunny, pleasant day. But now those clouds are just hanging there, taunting you. Hounding you. Pressuring you. Depressing you. Hurrying you up. Squeezing your schedule until you can never seem to cram enough work into the day to beat the rain that's coming. Or the dark that's coming. Or the change that's coming. Always something coming.

And so, when success—or at least our *definition* of success—proves elusive and out of reach, more trouble than it's worth, we tend to just quit on it. Let others have it. Then begrudge them for having it. Who cares? Probably wasn't meant for us anyway. Guess we just don't have what it takes to be successful.

Baloney.

And here's how I know it.

I've seen kids show up here at the Ranch, sometimes three or four at a time, dumped at our door by a parent or grandparent—believe it or not, on Christmas Eve. I've seen kids who at ten years old were already bearing the burden of raising their little brothers or sisters, practically single-handed. I've seen a girl who couldn't bring herself to eat supper with her new family for several days after she got here because back home she'd always been forced to "pay" for everything she ate (if you get my drift). For services rendered. I've seen a boy whose prior living arrangements let him spend only fifteen minutes a week with his mother and not to get any closer to her than from the front yard to the front porch. I've seen others who were victimized by being made to play roles in porn movies or were hired out to a neighbor on an as-requested basis in exchange for help with the rent and groceries only to be shamefully called a whore, a bitch, a liar, for just doing what they're told. I've seen kids who, if their parent were to walk into the room, might get up and land the first punch, just to get out ahead of the fighting. That's how violent the abuse had become in their home. I've seen more bruises and scar tissue and shattered innocence than I thought human beings were capable of dishing out, especially to children.

In fact, I actually don't know at this point if there's *anything* I haven't seen. If it can get any worse than what I've personally witnessed, even *I* would be shocked by it. And nothing much shocks me anymore.

But still I tell our kids—yes, *these* kids—again and again, "I know you're only eleven, or thirteen, or sixteen, or whatever—and you've already had *this, this,* and *this* happen to you. OK. So now where do you want to go? Because you can do it. It's in your hands to do something special with your life. We're here to help you, of course. And God said He's able to do more than you can ask or think or imagine. But first you've got to want it yourself. To be the best you can be."

And from what I've seen, success cannot be denied, even from those who've been denied every other advantage or opportunity. The road to success can begin at any point on the map with any person in the world.

Attainable success.

Not all of our kids, as you'd probably guess, choose to go this route. Some of them check out of here the minute they're legally free of our custody, and it's the last we hear from them again. Some buy in; some don't. But the ones that do, they soar to what I call success, no matter what anybody else might say.

Because whoever you are . . .

And whatever you've done . . .

However much you've seen or been mistreated in life . . .

Nothing can keep you from being successful.

Not where it counts.

So if you want to see me get a little worked up and out of sorts, just ask me this question—which I hear, on average, about every other day—"What's your success rate?"

"Well . . .

"Define success." That's always my first answer so you'd better be ready for it. If I told you one of the kids who grew up here with us was pulling down six figures as a business owner, would you tell me he or she had become a success? Because we've got those. Sure. But is that what I'm supposed to be looking for to determine whether we're making a difference in these children's lives—if they've got straight As in school, if they all graduate from college, if they're making enough money to pay off their mortgage?

Or does success actually show up in a much richer place than that? A place a lot more impressive than most people flippantly think?

Many years ago now I walked into my office, and a fifteen-year-old boy was sitting there. His face was bruised, his clothes were dirty, he smelled of sweat. You could tell it had been a bad week for him. Bad lifetime, most likely.

"Hey, Mr. John?" he said.

"How you doing, buddy? What's your name?"

Jeff. I'll call him Jeff.

"I sold my guitar yesterday morning to buy a bus ticket," he said, "and I've been riding all night. Then I walked clear over here from the bus station after I finally got dropped off. I came to ask you a question: would you give me the same chance you gave my sister?"

It's been a long time now since Jeff lived with us here at the Ranch. Hadn't heard from him in forever. I remember him graduating from high school. That's about the last I saw of him. But this past Father's Day I got a card in the mail. From Jeff. It came with a picture—of him along with his gorgeous wife and two handsome boys. Wish I could show that card to you right now so you could read what he wrote in it, but . . . trust me. It's strong.

Jeff, I assure you, showed up here with nothing. No guitar, no cigar. But he bought into what we were selling. And he took it and ran with it.

And Jeff, in my book, is a soaring success.

Show me a young man or woman who breaks the cycle; who puts out a strong effort on the job; is a source of love, caring, and provision in their family; and is faithful to God in their worship and lifestyle—and I'll show you somebody that I'll stand in front of any collection of people and say: "This is one of our boys. This is one of our girls. And I sure am proud of them."

Now if some of our kids don't quite get there, that doesn't mean I don't still believe in them. Doesn't mean I'd be ashamed for them to represent me or the Ranch. But I'm glad to say—and thankful to the Lord for it—I've had the pleasure of personally knowing hundreds of kids in my lifetime who've not been willing to let some hellaciously bad breaks define them as losers, quitters, or repeat perpetrators. I'm honored *by them* to see them standing with their families, being solid citizens, steadying out the path for a new generation.

And if that doesn't make Big Oak Ranch the best children's home in the nation, it's sure good enough for me.

What about you?

What would success look like in your life?

Don't Look Back

I think I've made it clear by now—and if I haven't, I'll put it out there for you again—I'm no model for how you do everything right. I often tell people when I go places to speak, "If you knew half the stuff I've done in my lifetime, you wouldn't have asked me here tonight." *Ha, ha.* They laugh. Always good for a laugh.

Let's be honest, though. If I knew half the stuff about *you*, I don't think you'd want me even as close to you as I am right now, sitting here (but not really here) on this book page. That's just the way we are. What we know about ourselves—sure, we're wise if *somebody* else knows it, who can help hold us accountable and shoot straight with us, somebody we can't snow or keep under the control of our little con game. But truthfully, not one of us is 100 percent crazy about who we've turned out to be in life. So anybody who acts like or looks like they've hardly ever made a strikeout, don't believe them. Play enough baseball, and it's just going to happen. Anybody who says they've never been thrown or kicked by a horse hasn't spent much time in the barn.

But when it comes to trying to be our best—even if we're fairly easy in admitting some of the rotten, embarrassing junk we've done—this backlog of regrets can slam the brakes on our forward progress if we let it. Our past mistakes can make us feel wholly inadequate for ever becoming much more than we've been in the past.

I've already mentioned it once, I believe, and I'm sure it won't be the last, since I think it's so crucial to being grounded and focused and comfortable with *who you are.* But this habit of looking too long in the rearview mirror, always checking behind you to see what's back there, gauging the view over your shoulder instead of the road out front—it's just not a good way to drive. The only thing it does is ensure that you'll keep on having additional, avoidable accidents. Or in too many cases, it's what keeps you from feeling like ever getting in the car and going *anywhere*. Stuck at home. Stuck in life.

People who've got "it" don't get stuck looking in their rearview mirror. Doesn't mean they don't check it regularly to see what they can learn from it, to pick up proper warnings and perspectives that might influence any decisions they need to make going forward. But they don't stay focused there. They don't camp there.

The rearview is not how they roll.

Truth is, and you know it, a lot of us pack up our regrets and take them with us every day, same as we pack our lunch, our billfold, and our cell phone. They're just always here, hanging around, crowding up the front seat, the backseat, the floor . . . any place they want to sit. We don't even try telling them to keep their feet off the dashboard or to shoo them off our desk when we get to work. And even if they run away and disappear for a little while, any old sight or sound could conjure them back up at any time. And suddenly, they're right here again—grabbing us by the hand and tugging us back to an earlier day, to a bad decision, a strained or lost relationship, an old pattern of sin.

Again, nothing wrong with letting past mistakes urge you forward, determined not to repeat the same stupidity that's cost you so much in terms of time, money, peace of mind, opportunity, whatever. But the day comes when you just can't keep looking back there behind you and expect the view to ever look any better. You've got to drop it and move on. You've got to kick it out of the car and drive off without it.

In my own line of work, I can think of times through the years when, for instance, I've given up on a kid too quickly. Overreacting to a really dumb mistake they made or being a little too rash and harsh in my judgment, I've made a snap decision. I've called their bluff. I've told them they've used up their last chance to stay here. And I've meant it. Sometimes, frankly, in order to protect the other kids we've promised to care for and defend, taking this action is the appropriate, tough-love, but difficult choice to make. But in some cases I can look back now and see where I forced it. Flubbed it. One child in particular I can think of—if someone were just to mention her first name right now to my daughter Reagan or me, we'd, uh . . . we'd feel it. In our gut. Still hurts. Wrong call.

Others, in hindsight, we probably gave them more chances than we should, to the detriment of our other kids and even to the detriment of themselves. My patience and desire for them to pull through and push past it went on longer than it should. They'd have been better served if I'd seen what was happening sooner so I could've gotten them the kind of help they really needed.

Regrets. We've all got 'em.

Somebody asked Coach Bryant one time, "When you think back on what you did to help so many good athletes become great players—the Joe Namaths, the Kenny Stablers, the list goes on and on—how do you feel about that?"

He said, "I don't think about them. I think instead about the players I somehow couldn't get through to, the ones I didn't know how to reach, didn't know which buttons to push to make them excel. Great talents, good players, but I lost them or ran them off."

Regret.

I get it. I've done it. Kids I was too soft on. Kids I was too rough on. Kids I didn't know how to handle, and so I ended up not doing what they truly needed me to do for them.

But I learned a long time ago, if I let those failures keep eating me alive every day, I won't be able to be present and on point with the kids who are sitting right here in front of me. I'll perpetuate a pattern of missteps and inconsistency. I'll act on fear instead of clear focus. And so I'll only succeed at making things worse. I'll just be building that wall of regret even higher than it already was. Not that I'll never wince again at what happened back then, but not so much that it throws me off balance for handling the next situation that's coming up.

Something inside us feels . . . better? more responsible? . . . if we're walking around sufficiently punishing ourselves for doing the wrong thing. And, sure, taking ownership of it is good. Admitting failure is smart. Mature. But if we keep on kicking ourselves, not being willing to move beyond it, the person we used to be in the past feels entitled to maintain far too much volume in our heads, compared to the God who says, "Behold, I make all things new" (Rev. 21:5 KJV).

Failure is actually, and ironically, a key component of success. Henry Ford, the industrial genius behind the first mass-produced automobile, was well-known for saying, "The only real mistake is the one from which we learn nothing" because "even a mistake," he also said, "may turn out to be the one thing necessary for achievement."

Simon Peter, we know, became one of the pillars of the early church. An amazing man of faith, courage, and inspiration. But one of the ways he got there was through one of the most famous failures in all the Bible, denying that he even knew who Jesus was, after spending three whole years at His side. As bold and headstrong as he'd always been, Peter ran scared when the heat was on.

It happens. You hate it.

But you build on it. You don't get buried in it.

The past, as poorly as yours or mine may appear from today's perspective, is not a place we can afford to live, not if we hold out any hope for soaring to our full potential. As disappointing or defeating as your regrets may be, as many ways as they may conspire to confine you to the sidelines, you can't let them call the shots from behind you. Just can't.

And if this feels like nothing but another pep talk— a motivational speech that sounds all guns ablazing at the moment, but you don't think it'll hold water later on in the trenches—remember that God has promised not only to "go before you," leading you forward into battle, but also to be "your rear guard," covering your flank from sneak attack (Isa. 52:12 NASB). If He can fling your sins "as far as the east is from the west" (Ps. 103:12), surely He knows how far south to take even your worst, heaviest regrets so they can never again affect your northbound progress.

There's a reason your windshield is a whole lot bigger than your rearview mirror. And a reason you can't drive in reverse. Forget your regrets and keep going.

Time Travel

Two things I hope you take from this chapter: (1) you can't soar to success as long as you're mired in where you've been. Bitterness, excuses, and regrets never come together into anything worthwhile. They can dig a lot of holes but not the kind that turn into footings for new construction.

Then there's this: (2) your future success is not even limited by your future.

Somewhere in the back of our heads, a clock is ticking. And like the wall clocks that may be in your house, you don't always hear the steady rhythm of the second hands, their sound being drowned out by the other demanding noise of the day. Or you may notice the pounding so loudly sometimes that it keeps you awake, nearly drives you crazy.

But either way, whether you hear it or not, the clock ticks on. Second by second. Never stopping. Always ticking.

And so every morning's newspaper (like clockwork) includes a full page or two of little write-ups—some with a formal head shot, some without—each of them announcing the recent death of a local citizen or someone with ties to the area. He was seventy-one, the obituary says. She was eighty-eight. Or fifty-four. Occasionally even nineteen or thirty. But they average out to a number that, when compared with the age of the nose on your face, can cause your ears to perk up, becoming aware of a ticking clock in the background. And though you hadn't really been noticing it right then, you can sure hear it now . . . winding down on you.

But no, it's not.

Not really.

As believers in Christ, of course, death has already been transformed for us by the undeserved grace of God into nothing but a grand doorway to eternal life, a freeing relief from all the toil and trouble. "Death, where is your victory? Death, where is your sting?" (1 Cor. 15:55). But truly, no one's future is really over when their mortal life is over. We can each live on through the investments we make in other people.

So there's no need to restrict your life's work to sixty, eighty, a hundred years—whatever time God gives you on the earth. No need for feeling constantly hustled up and running behind. Because when you pour yourself into serving and equipping others, the path of your soaring trajectory takes off and doesn't show any signs of slowing down anytime soon.

I'm sitting here right now, for instance, sixty some-odd years into my lifespan and forty years into a calling that's become the Big Oak Ranch we see today. But in reality the arc and reach of this place has only just begun. Because when I first cranked it up in 1974, I didn't set it to self-destruct as soon as my days of working it were over. I mean, I was obviously too young to really think about it that way or recognize it at the time, but through the years I've increasingly understood that God was building something here a lot bigger and longer lasting than this gnarly old body of mine that I carry around with me every day. This is *His* work, *His* building. I'm caretaking it for my little stretch of the race, but the finish line is nowhere near in sight.

And so for me this involves a relay. A relay of knowledge and leadership. Of trust and release. And, I daresay, the same

is true for you. Whatever you do, wherever you go, and whoever you influence, the drive to be your best joins hands with
the drive to help others be their best as well. And as you keep
relaying what you've learned and what you can offer to those
around you, you're quietly becoming a better you than even *you*
are capable of being. You're living for a future that outlives you.
You're playing in a sandbox of success that you don't need to
leave behind just because it's sundown or suppertime.

You can play on.

And that's exactly what I'm getting to do today, through
two of my favorite people in the world, who just happen to be
the two people God has led home to the Ranch to carry it into
the future.

My son Brodie was working as a successful partner in a land
and timber real estate business, after a long athletic career that
ended up taking him to the NFL, when God directed his path
back to the Ranch. And my daughter Reagan was enjoying success as a wife, a mom, and a career in the counseling profession
when the Lord led her back here as well, to become our child-
care team director. Neither one of them had orchestrated their
lives to make an automatic return trip home. This wasn't like a
grand master plan we'd worked up ahead of time. But God, in
the astounding wisdom of His will—along with, I'm sure, a little
assistance from my wife's prayers—drew our kids to return here
as young adults, as well-equipped leaders. And part of my joy
today is working with them in taking the Ranch to new, longer,
brighter avenues of potential.

I used to do everything around here. I cleaned out the sew-
ers. Dug the field lines. Cleared the property and grounds.
Handled the intake of new children. Hired the houseparents.
Led the meetings. Supervised the office. And then, after I'd
showered and cleaned up a little from all of that, I often went
out to speak somewhere at night. Between Tee and me, we put in
some long days and sometimes even longer nights. Always had

great staff. Great people around us. And faithful people to support us. As best we could, we did it all for the glory of God and the opportunity to change children's lives for the better.

But again, being the best means not getting hung up in the past, even in the good parts, in the hard work and measurable progress you may see when you're looking back on it. Being your best means being bold enough to look forward and embrace change and to relinquish some of the control you believe to be so essential to making things work the way they should.

I remember a day a number of years ago when I moved my office from the boys' ranch to the girls' ranch, a twenty-minute drive away. And before I left, God and I had a little talk. I told Him everything I could think of. I asked Him to forgive me for every poor action and attitude I'd set into motion from my seat in that place. "But God," I said, "when I walk out of here, I never intend to sit in this office again." And I haven't been back to try taking it over or even sit in the Boys' Ranch director's chair in more than sixteen years.

You can't keep being everything. Only a fool refuses to loosen his grip on certain responsibilities so those areas can grow and blossom and become even better in others' hands. Remember, the pot-bound plant will only grow as large as the size of the pot it's planted in.

So let that clock just keep ticking away, trying to scare you into submission, counting down the hours on your influence and effectiveness. But instead of letting it turn you into a pile of worthless regrets and missed opportunities—which, again, all of us can stack up as high as we care to build them—let it propel you even further into the future than you've perhaps been aware enough to contemplate. By giving, by teaching, by mentoring, by sacrificing, by thinking of somebody besides yourself for a change, you can lay some charges of spiritual dynamite in the ground that will still be exploding and breaking up obstacles for people, even when you're nowhere around anymore.

You and I, the way I see it, can choose to live either one of two ways: *regrettable* or *incredible*. Which way do you plan to take it? By choosing to live in regret, you'll never be forward-looking enough to reach anywhere near your full potential. You'll constantly find yourself bumping up against choke points your fears or insecurities won't let you pass through. But by choosing the other path, even with new mistakes and miscalculations to be made every day, you'll be setting yourself on a steady trajectory of excellence and significance. When you goof up, you'll hear God saying: "Come on, son, you're better than this. I didn't create you for this. I created you for incredible greatness." Instead of getting hung up in your imperfections, you'll push through them on your way to bigger game and better days. Instead of measuring your success rate by seeing how it squares with everybody else's, you'll march to the individual drumbeat God has uniquely patterned into *who you are*. And you'll find your joy from knowing He's doing His thing in you as you give it your all, simply doing your best at what He's told you to do.

A few months ago Tee and I were out for supper at one of our finer dining establishments around here: Huddle House. If you've ever driven through the South or midwestern America, you've probably seen signs for them, like maybe at the next exit off a major highway. Ah, I can hear the plates clattering right now, hear the waitress asking me, "Honey," if I'd like a refill on my coffee. Think country fried steak. Mushroom gravy. Mashed potatoes, green beans, and a thick slice of buttery Texas toast on the side. Or if you're feeling like it, why not a full-on breakfast? Anytime. Day or night.

Get the picture? Feel the fat grams?

We're walking inside, I'm holding the door for a young lady, when she looks up at me and says, "Well, *hey* there."

"Mary? Is that you? How you doing, baby?"

She had come to us years before from a horrible childhood. I remember so clearly one time, out driving somewhere with her and a few of the other kids, she had leaned over and pointed to a motel we were passing. "Look over there, Mr. John," she said. "That's where my mama used to leave me." To do God knows what.

But today? Mary's not the little girl anymore with the abuse and abandonment issues. "I'm doing good," she told me. "I've got two kids. Married. Everything's good."

She's doing good.

And because of that, so am I.

Soaring good.

Tee and I went and sat down. Ordered, ate, finished up our dinner. Then when time came for us to go, and the waitress began clearing our plates away, I asked if she had our check ready.

"Oh, it's covered, Mr. Croyle."

"Huh?"

"Your meal's been taken care of."

"What? By who?"

"That lady who was sitting at that table over there. She paid it for you."

Get out.

The next time I see Mary—and here's hoping there *is* a next time—I'm going to fuss at her good for doing something like that . . . right before I hug her neck and thank her to pieces for making my day that evening, for showing Mrs. Tee and me such a kind, touching gesture. I went home that night realizing, when you get right down to it, everything I'd ever wanted when I started up the Ranch—when I'd first said I wanted it to be the best children's home in America—was to see exactly what I saw at our friendly neighborhood Huddle House on a friendly neighborhood weeknight. I saw a child who'd become a responsible young adult, making her way in the world, raising her family in a stable home environment, and learning how to give back, even with everything that had once been taken away from her. She had finally broken the cycle from where she'd come.

Let everybody else have whatever they want to call success. Me—I'll take watching God do something like turn a little girl's whole future right side up and give us the privilege of being there to watch it happen.

Which one of my regrets would've been worth nursing, costing me the chance to be part of the much bigger plans God had set apart for me? And which one of my tomorrows am I going to squander on myself or my worries instead of trusting that giving my best and giving it to others won't pay off a whole lot better than I could ever imagine?

Let loose. Let go.

And let's soar.

CHAPTER 5

Fight

You're a Warrior

The longer he spoke, the quieter the room became. No one reaching for their water glass. No one clearing their throat or scratching an imaginary itch on their face. And it wasn't like, you know, some spiritually convicting church service or anything, where the preacher was coming down hard on a particularly damning subject, and everybody was too afraid to make a move for fear of looking guilty. Nor was it a school assembly with a bunch of impressionable, young twelve- to fourteen-year-olds, kids whose life experiences were still in the formative stages, who could still be easily mesmerized by what a guy like this was saying.

Instead, as I looked around the room, which was packed to capacity with seven or eight hundred people, I saw the likes of Pat Dye (former head football coach and athletic director at Auburn), Gene Stallings (former Alabama and NFL head coach), John Cooper (Ohio State), R. C. Slocum (Texas A&M), Gus Malzahn (currently at Auburn), Bo Jackson (multisport superstar of the 1980s and '90s). I'm talking about *that* kind of audience. And almost to a man, they were all just leaning forward, eyes hardly blinking—perhaps afraid that if they *did* move, this guy might call them out from the platform and want a word with them in the parking lot afterward.

Brodie said to me as we were leaving, "I don't know if that was the *worst* speaker I've ever heard or the *best* one"—because, admittedly, he didn't deliver his address with a lot of charisma or stage flair. No warm-up gags or rehearsed jokes. He was just like, "So that's my story. Thanks for your time." Yet at the *same* time it was riveting, powerful, unforgettable. And I'm pretty sure I wasn't the only one in the building that night who felt that way—or who said on their way out, something like, "Just give me a skirt to wear. I only *thought* I knew what it meant to be a man."

The speaker's name was Marcus Luttrell. If you've heard of him from his best-selling book *Lone Survivor*, or from the recent feature film of the same name, starring Mark Wahlberg, then you already know his death-defying story from the rugged mountain passes of Afghanistan, wartime in June 2005. Dispatched as part of a four-man unit of Navy SEALs to locate and perhaps capture (or kill, if it came to that) a key leader of the Taliban, they were inserted into position by helicopter under cloak of darkness, awaiting their chance to spot this valuable target. Once the warlord's precise coordinates and operation could be ascertained through their on-the-ground reconnaissance, they were to radio back to headquarters with the information—prepare to rain down fire from the sky.

I won't retell the whole account, but basically their cover was blown by (of all things) a straggling band of goatherds, grazing along the high-country mountain face. And because of an unexpected, unexplainable failure in their communication gear, which left them unable to notify their command unit of the situation, they made the fateful decision to let the men go rather than kill them in cold blood.

Tough call. Impossible call. Decisions made in live combat are usually that way, not between good and bad but between bad and worse. And whether or not the decision they made was the best among all available options, I'll leave it to brighter military minds than my own to figure out. My only real experience with war is the two-player card game that goes by that name. And I've barely got the reflexes and math skills to deal with that, so . . .

All I know is what Marcus told us that night. How they came under fire from Taliban warriors, who had obviously been alerted to their presence by the spooked herdsmen. How they desperately tried to hold their ground against dozens, perhaps hundreds of heavily armed gunmen—four brave Americans, ridiculously outnumbered in the fight of their lives on foreign terrain. How the bullets rang and enemies fell to their right and left, all while Marcus and his men were falling backwards, farther downhill, tumbling and skidding and breaking bones on rock ledges and fallen tree logs but still shooting, still hitting.

The deafening battle continued for forty-five minutes or more. Constant gunfire. Rocket-propelled grenades. Shards of rock and earth raining onto their positions.

I guess I just really didn't know the kind of fighting heroics some guys are actually, honestly capable of performing. He told of one SEAL brother, Danny, who died in his arms, shot in the face while Marcus was trying to carry him to safety. But before the kill shot landed, Danny had already sustained at least four or five gunshot wounds—one that took off his right thumb while he was holding the radio, one through his lower back and out through his stomach, two to his neck and throat, maybe more.

And yet even while being dragged bodily downhill, covered in blood, he was still loading and firing, loading and firing.

He told of another SEAL, nicknamed Axe, who with a sniper's accuracy had continued to pick off the fiery, turbaned shooters from a distance—until a bullet sliced open his own head, blinding him, inflicting a ghastly brain wound. Yet by the time Marcus could reach him, Axe was still trying to bandage himself up, trying to work his pistol—his only weapon left. When rescuers finally found his body, several unspent cartridges were still clutched in his hand. It appeared from best conjecture that the enemy had needed to cut his head off to make him stop fighting.

And then there was Mike, who, despite taking a direct hit to the back, blood pouring from its exit path through his chest, made the daring move to step out into a clearing and dial HQ from his mobile phone—a last resort they'd vetoed earlier after their radio had gone dead, not wanting the transmission signal to give away their scouting location. This last-ditch maneuver on Mike's part was ultimately what saved Marcus's life because it made their superiors aware of possible survivors from the doomed mission. But by placing himself at such an exposed angle, thirty yards uphill from where Marcus was spraying cover fire, Mike had no real chance against the crazed peppering of AK-47s, strobing and strafing his unguarded position.

This is where—as the speaker recounted the events of that day to the crowd that evening—you could see him actively reliving it all in his mind. *"Marcus! Marcus!"* his buddy had yelled out in final agony, "Help me, Marcus! Please help me!" That's the chilling, echoing scream that still wakes him in the night. Still haunts him out of nowhere. "At that moment," he said, "I was a coward. Laid down my gun in a gunfight. Had to cover my ears because my best friend was up the mountain, and I couldn't get to him. I couldn't save him. He was my family. My brother. Dying.

"I'm sorry, y'all," he said. "I was a coward."

Well, I don't think so. Do you? Neither did Coach Dye, Coach Stallings, Bo Jackson—none of them.

But what about you? What about me?

Are *we*? Cowards?

When it's time to fight, do we know how to strap it on and show no fear? No quit? Make no excuses and take no prisoners?

You and I may have walked away from a few fights through the years, from struggles we should've taken up, from missions that called for active duty, not passive acceptance. Because life is a battle. The Bible says so. People are in danger. Our survival and the survival of those we love and care about are at stake and under constant threat.

So like it or not, there's only one position to take if we expect to emerge alive and intact from the conflicts coming against us—conflicts from the world, from the flesh, from the devil, from everywhere. The crosshairs are painted bright red on our hearts and on our heads, on our homes and on our honor. Some of us may not be warriors by nature, but we're in a war nonetheless.

And we must fight.

To the death.

To Protect and Defend

Tommy was fifteen—one of our first boys here at the Ranch, way back in the early days—when I got a call from a certain woman who had a complaint about him. This lady's daughter and our Tommy went to the same school together, and she, as a mother, was concerned about some inappropriate things he had written to the girl.

To say she was "concerned" is actually putting it mildly.

And, frankly, I was pretty ticked about it myself. This obviously wasn't the kind of thing I was willing to tolerate in any of our boys. So I went to Tommy, told him what I'd heard, and asked if it was true. And then he

"Yes, sir, it is." And then he told me the whole story.

"Well, I appreciate you being honest with me about it," I said, "for telling me the truth. But here's the deal. You're going to have to take the medicine because what you did was wrong."

"I know it," he said.

"And this girl's mother wants to come over here—*tonight*— to talk about it. And I've told her she can come. I'll be here to defend you, of course. But I can't defend what you've done. After that, we'll see what we need to do."

When evening rolled around, the woman showed up at the house, accompanied not only by her daughter but also by her own father. Triangulation maneuver, I guess. Her objective, it seemed, was not only to file her list of grievances but apparently to lock Tommy up in the filing cabinet. Dead or alive. Throw away the key.

"Now there's one rule, ma'am," I said, as we all sat nervously down. "You can't touch him. You can say anything you want to say but don't put a hand on him."

Don't worry. She didn't need to.

By the time she finally pulled back and the ringing stopped in my ears, I thought I might need to call the paramedics. Not for me, not for Tommy, but for *her*. She was sweating, panting, veins still raised on her neck and her temples. She had amply defended her daughter from the crude vocabulary of an adolescent boy. Good for her. Nobody could fault her for that, even if I'm sure she could've communicated the same amount of information with far less fireworks and theatrics.

"Thank you, ma'am," I said, as her breathing began to normalize a bit. "Trust me, I do hear what you're saying. The boy messed up. Bad. And I'm going to discipline him severely, I promise you."

"What you *should* do is—"

"But before I do anything," I interrupted, "I'd like to show you something else." At that I reached beside me and pulled out a sheaf of letters her daughter had written to Tommy and said, "You might want to read these first . . . to see if he's the *only* one who needs some correcting."

She looked at her daughter, whose face had suddenly bleached to a chalky pale, looked back at me, and then snatched the small stack of letters from my hand. She was certain there couldn't be anything incriminating inside.

To this day that woman won't speak to me. The last interaction we ever had was seeing her yanking up her daughter, head-motioning to her dad, and storming out the door.

And just like that, the wall paint, which had somehow managed not to peel away from the sheetrock during the reaming-out of the past half hour, breathed a thankful sigh of relief. And Tommy and I remained as the only people left in the room—him, still seated in a chair, and me, having risen to stand while the lady and her entourage were exiting the premises.

Amid the shock of an uneasy silence, Tommy stood slowly to his feet, walked over toward me, and did something fifteen-year-old Tommys, who come from backgrounds and upbringings like his, simply don't do.

He hugged me.

Father to son.

And said in words I've never forgotten: "No one's ever stood up for me before."

We see this and hear this so often from our kids here at the Ranch. All their life, for the most part, all they've known are people who bailed on them. People who put themselves and their own desires first. People who didn't seem to notice or care that their child was under duress, in trouble, needing help, and buckling under the weight. In some cases—in *many* cases—these people were in fact the very individuals the child needed defending from the most.

But even if your children are not at risk from anyone's cruelty or unkindness at home, like many of our kids often were, they're still out there with battles to fight. With bullies that make sport of their perceived weaknesses. With cultural expectations that play havoc with their self-esteem. With injustices that can deeply hurt, even if some of those blows must simply be endured as part of life in an unfair world. And as their parent, you need to see yourself as their fighter. As their defender. The one who holds their tender heart squarely in the palm of your hand . . . and protects them.

I'm not saying, of course, that you should turn into the mom or dad who hounds the coach or teacher or group leader for not recognizing the obvious superiority of your child's ability and for not giving them more playing time (or whatever the case may be). I'm not saying you can, or should, always be out there fighting their battles for them. Part of growing up and maturing is learning how to handle some of these disputes and disappointments in their lives in a brave, levelheaded manner. And yet they still need to know you're there to listen and recognize what's going on, to be attentive to the condition of their soul, and when necessary, to *fight* in their corner. To rally to their cause.

Same thing goes for marriage—especially husbands fighting for their wives (not fighting *with* them, fighting *for* them). I often tell our girls, "I want you to find husbands who are real men—men who will defend you, the way the men here at the Ranch defend you."

Perhaps your inborn temperament as a husband is quiet and unassuming. Perhaps your nerve endings typically go out of their way to avoid conflict. You may or may not be the kind of guy who wades into confrontations when necessary with a gritty stare, a pointed word, and a tough chin. But if your wife is coming under attack—physically, emotionally, spiritually, with maybe her reputation or integrity being clouded by speculation—you'd better be ready to spring into some kind of action.

Take her side. Speak your piece. Go to bat for her. And always be praying for her.

Stand in the gap. And fight.

Until it's simply *who you are.*

I'm proud to say I see this brand of toughness in my son Brodie. I'll even go out on a limb and say I see it in my son-in-law, John David. Hard for a dad to admit it sometimes, when he gives his daughter to another man, but in J. D.'s case—very true.

And if I didn't know it before what happened in Florida that summer, I sure know it now.

Brodie had taken his two older nephews, Cade and Will, ages eight and six at the time, out beyond a sandbar in the gulf to dive for sand dollars . . . at their nagging, persistent request. You should know that swimming in the ocean is not Brodie's (or Reagan's) favorite thing to do. In fact, there's not much of anything about the beach those two actually like—not the jam-packed crowds of people, not the sand, not the taste or feel of salt water. And definitely not the threat of sharks.

Should never have let 'em see *Jaws* at too early an age.

J. D. and Reagan were also out there in the water but closer to the shoreline, a little less than chest deep, holding their two-year-old son, Gibbs, while Uncle Brodie monitored the older boys on a raft, farther out. At one point, watching from a distance, J. D. spotted a fin as it was skimming out of the water, no more than fifteen yards beyond the trough where Brodie was currently bobbing. "Hey, look, boys! A dolphin!" he hollered out to them. Brodie, spinning around, poked his head under to see if he could spot the big fish through his goggles. Sure enough, there it was.

Only it wasn't a dolphin.

Definitely . . . not . . . a dolphin.

When the dorsal fin appeared again, J. D. realized what Brodie had already discovered. They were well within the striking range of a ten-foot hammerhead.

Better do something. Fast.

"All right, guys," Brodie said, not trying to freak the boys out, "I need y'all to get your legs up on the raft. We're swimming in. We're going to be fine, but I need you to do what I say, OK?" Meanwhile, J. D. was shoving little Gibbs at Reagan, saying, "Run! Go! Get in!"

And here's where—if you'll excuse a little break in the action—I want to be sure to frame up how this story fits into *your* life, not just the lives of my grown kids and their families.

Sharks come in all shapes and sizes with the clear intent of eating you, your spouse, and your children. Some arrive as threats on your family's time together and your schedule. Others threaten to bring harm into your home through godless, degrading entertainment or excessive online exposure. They can take the form of unhealthy friendships and relationships, of reckless spending, of spiritual threats to everyone's faith and unity. You name it. Some are subtle temptations, barely visible to the naked eye until they're already bearing down on you, doing their damage. Some, on the other hand, are all too highly predictable, readily avoidable. And yet because of some risky behavior and careless actions, you or some members of your family may find yourselves in an active danger zone, having foolishly drifted back out into shark-infested waters.

As husbands, fathers—as wives and mothers too—you possess several options whenever a shark has moved into attack position against your family. You can (1) bail, outrunning your spouse or children to the shore, concerned only about your own skin; (2) stand there and do nothing, paralyzed, overwhelmed; or (3) move toward the problem, directly into its eyeballs, straight at the nose on its wicked face.

What'll it be?

One, two, or three?

J. D. pushed my daughter and grandson toward safety and then knifed his way back out into deep water. Toward the monster. To rescue his two other boys.

By the time he reached them, the shark had actually circled them all, and it now lurked visibly in the shallower water. So when it made its turn back out, my son and son-in-law were standing directly between the shark and the two boys behind them on the float.

In the gap. In defense.

Now Brodie, despite *hating* sharks, actually has (or at least *had*) a curious fascination with them. The Discovery Channel's *Shark Week* was always a television fixture each year during NFL training camp in August, so he routinely caught some of the episodes at night whenever there was some downtime. And one of the things he'd learned from watching those programs is that when a shark is preparing to attack, it'll show its fin at first and then dive underneath to strike from the bottom.

Sure enough, that's exactly what was playing out in front of them. The fin, the dive, the whole killing match. The textbook tactic. The two guys remember saying to each other, out loud, "This is really happening, man"—and thinking to themselves, *I guess this is it. I'm about to be eaten by a shark.*

At seven or eight yards away, the fin submerged. Its shadowy body approached. Seconds later its nose was a scant three feet in front of them. Closing in. Then for whatever reason, it veered sharply to the right, swimming past them into open water, near enough that they could feel its momentum and sensation around their feet. But before it had a chance to circle again for another sortie, they'd splashed and shoved and high-stepped to the knee-deep water and finally up onto the beach sand.

Safe.

Protected. Defended.

Even our oldest grandson, Cade, had an arm around his little brother, telling him, "It's going to be OK, Will. I won't let anything happen to you."

Isn't that awesome? That's what I'm talking about. Taking on the sharks. Putting yourself between your family and their enemies. Laying down your life, being willing to die, if that's what it takes to protect their hearts, minds, and bodies.

No child or woman alive wouldn't kill for a father or husband like that.

A fighter.

Hard Day's Life

Life, ready or not, is full of hard things. Sharks are just the beginning. Hate to break it to you like that if you were wishing otherwise. But I'm not a wizened, old cynic or fatalist who's saying this to you. It's just the truth. Life's hard. And generally keeps getting harder as you go along. So one of the worst things you can do is not to realize this, expect it, and prepare for it.

Prepare to fight.

Part of what makes life so hard is just the everyday struggle. And depending on where you are—your age, marital status, family size, health condition, any of a hundred different factors—these struggles will vary from person to person, even from year to year and decade to decade.

At one point, for instance, during the first nine months of running the Ranch, I didn't draw a paycheck. We lived on my wife's $500 a month salary. Gross. (You can take that word any way you want to take it.) But that was all. So we know what it's like to play from behind financially. I had to make a few phone calls sometimes, asking certain people to whom we owed money, "Can you give me thirty days?" God was faithful, of course. Many times we gathered our family and staff together and prayed for a miracle, for a certain dollar figure. And more than once the money showed up as if out of nowhere—cash in the mailbox—just like it happens on *The 700 Club*. Except it was happening to us, not in a made-for-TV testimonial.

But sometimes God decided that what we apparently needed most was to trust Him even more, beyond those thirty days. And so we learned what it was like to have the power cut off. Not fun. Life is tough. It can bite.

But the people I admire most in the Bible and throughout history are men and women who were fighters, not fretters, folks who muscled through the one-after-another challenges of life with hope, hard work, contentment, and optimism. "A worker's appetite works for him," the proverb says, "because his hunger urges him on" (Prov. 16:26). I like that. We should be glad, actually, that God doesn't magically exempt us from every experience that involves shortage and strain, struggle and sacrifice. Otherwise, we would forget where our power and supply truly come from. We'd think we somehow cracked the code on trouble-free living through our own smarts and initiative (see Ps. 59:11). Better to stay hungry and fight, the Bible seems to be saying, than to go soft through a lack of resistance training. So until we're finally with Him in heaven, the battle fatigues ought always to be hanging in the closet, ready to go.

Speaking of military wear, life calls not only for *physical* battle but also for *spiritual* battle. And therefore, it calls for spiritual armor and weaponry—like truth and faith and Scripture and prayer. Spiritual warfare, seen for many years primarily as the spooky doctrine of charismatics and Pentecostals, is not just a mystical creep show we'd rather not think about—too weird, too out there. It's simply a biblically revealed reality. "Our battle is not against flesh and blood," wrote Paul the apostle, "but against the rulers, against the authorities, against the world powers of this darkness, against the spiritual forces of evil in the heavens" (Eph. 6:12).

Ask our houseparents, and they'll tell you. They hear the demons. I'm not one of those guys, you know, who sees an evil spirit behind every sticker bush. Neither are they. But I've talked with numerous housemoms and dads who tell me, "I've walked down the hallway at night, and I've heard the moans in the children's sleep"—not demon possession or anything but kids who've seen too much, heard too much, and been opened to too much not to sometimes be tormented by the memories, twitching in the darkness.

It's devilish. It's cruel.

And it's not as far under the surface as we'd like to think. For any of us.

We all, as Christian believers, are relentlessly opposed by spiritual darkness. We feel it. We see it. We hear it—in our heads, in our habits, in our interactions with others, in all kinds of places, expected and unexpected. Thank God we can overcome it and prevail against it, that we can experience freedom and confidence and victory in Jesus. But not without a fight.

Life is just hard. It comes with migraines and traffic tie-ups. With plumbing repairs and knee replacements. With critics and haters. Every so often it even comes with a loss to Auburn in the Iron Bowl. (Not enough to mention, really, but on those rare occasions when it happens, you do kind of feel like wanting to fight somebody.)

But all kidding aside—if you hang around long enough, you'll come across some of those crossroads where you're forced to make some monumentally hard decisions, like the kind that cropped up on Marcus Luttrell and company in the battlefield. And you may not ever really know, this side of eternity, if you made the right call, if you said the right thing. But you've got to keep fighting, pressing forward.

Try looking into the eyes of a twelve-year-old girl, for instance, who says to you, "Let me get this straight. God is everywhere, right?"

Yes.

"He loves me and wants to protect me."

Yes.

"He's my Father."

Yes.

"Then where in the world was He when my daddy was hurting me? You say God was there. Why didn't He stop him?"

Forty years later I still don't have a definitive answer for that one—at least not an answer that can totally clear it up in a little girl's mind.

Or try talking to a nineteen-year-old boy, as I've done, who can't seem to keep himself out of trouble and who tells you he's blowing this joint and taking off on his own. You know he doesn't have any place to go. You know he'll probably just end up getting a girl pregnant somewhere, if not finding himself crossways with the law and getting his rear end thrown in jail. In all our forty years of doing this, I've never heard one single person say, "The best thing that ever happened to me was the day I left the Ranch." And yet here's one itching to leave. Sure enough, you can't hold a space any longer for somebody who won't abide by the rules. There's another boy over here who wants the opportunity this one can't appear to appreciate. So you just come out and say it, "OK, fine. You're old enough to leave? Then leave." But that's a tough day for me, for all of us— because we know it's just the beginning of a *lot* of tough days for a kid who knows better yet doesn't know what he doesn't know.

And then there's a situation like Natalie's, who came to live with us at age five, along with her big sister. Lived here fourteen years. And always struggled. Never really adjusted or settled in. Not all the way, at least. She was one of those kids I kept worrying about, trying to figure out how to get through to her.

One sad morning, though—one of the hardest mornings you can imagine—I stood beside her hospital bed. The doctor said her nineteen-year-old brain was spaghetti, that the car accident from two nights ago had rendered her a vegetable, that she'd never be any better than the condition I was looking at, completely comatose and hooked up to a breathing machine.

As he was talking, my mind flared backward to a memory of her, when she was, oh, nine years old, I guess. She'd hopped up in my lap on a bus ride back to school, when we were all coming home from a ball game, and asked me a question: "Are you always going to be there for me?"

"Absolutely. Always."

"You promise?" she said, cocking her head to one side.

I paused, wanting to make sure she really heard me this time.

"I promise, Natalie. I promise. I will *always* be here for you."

And here I was. Her *mom and dad* weren't there, same as they'd *never* been there. In all those fourteen years, never saw them once. So it was just me, holding her hand, while her older sister was across from me, holding the other. Her mom was in prison; her dad was . . . wherever. But not here. We were all the family she had.

Her big sister and I had to make the call. To end her life.

That made the *fourth time* I've stood in that impossible position . . . as a father or as a son. And it never gets any easier, only more tragic. Within the horrifying fifteen minutes or so (usually) when the machine quits sending breathing impulses to the brain, and the body eventually can't keep up its involuntary reflexes without smothering, you watch death move in and life move out. It's horrible. With pain on my face, I leaned down close to hers and quietly said, "I'll see you later, baby." And I know I will.

But, *man,* in the moment—that's hard.

Yet you keep going. And keep battling. You keep your focus, your loyalty, your persistence, your trustworthiness.

We're always left with a choice, whenever life is meaner and tougher than we wish it to be. Roll over and quit? Give in to ourselves? Get worked up into spin cycles of fear and worry? Grouse and complain about how unfair it all is? Douse it in alcohol or pain meds or some other form of escapism?

Or fight . . .

Keep fighting . . .

I'm no elite fighting machine—no Navy SEAL, no Army Ranger, no Green Beret, no Delta Force operative. But I hope you're hearing me loud and clear today, listening close enough that you could hear a pin drop. Because if our homes and families need anything today, it's people who won't lie down when life is hard. People who will do the right thing and do it with courage.

Tell me that's *who you are* . . . or who you're committed now to be.

CHAPTER 6

Trust

You've Got What You Need

We've looked at a lot of things so far that can help you (and me) become the people we're fully capable of being—no matter where you come from, no matter how much you've been struggling lately, no matter what you felt like this morning when you got up or what kept you awake and maybe troubled in the night.

For one thing, be sure you're staying *focused*, remember?—not spraying bullets at everything that pops its head up. That only succeeds at draining energy from your tank and drawing you away from what makes you so uniquely special, away from the gifts God has built into you and wants to maximize through your life.

You've also got to think *long-term*—not judging yourself by the limited sample size of life experiences you've accumulated so far but considering yourself on a marathon . . . mile three, mile five, mile ten . . . keeping on chugging, doing the work, establishing healthy patterns and commitments for the long haul.

You've got to want to be your absolute *best*—setting high standards of integrity, character, and achievement, while being sure, though, not to let others steal your joy and contentment if your version of success doesn't exactly square with what they think it ought to be.

And, of course, you've got to *fight*—not shying away or being surprised by the rugged realities of life but sailing into each day with a fierce resolve to do battle for what really matters. And especially to make any sacrifice necessary to protect and defend your family.

I've got a lot more of these pointers to lay out there for you, of course, before we're done. Get me talking, and I could go on like this for hours. All these years of raising children has taught me more than I know how to catalog, in terms of what it takes to keep growing and prospering, pushing past the inevitable obstacles of life that try to keep you washed out and washed up. I've seen it at work in enough of these kids, in fact, as well as in many other people I've known, that I'm convinced it's possible for anybody.

So I know "it" when I see it.

I think you do too.

And I want one of those people with "it" to be you. And me.

I've seen it, for example, in a young man I'll introduce to you as Michael. He was only six years old when his daddy dropped him off here at the Ranch, along with his two brothers, just two days before Christmas. Talk about wrecking the holidays for your kids. But his father's new girlfriend had laid down an ultimatum: "It's either me or those stupid boys." Couldn't have both. And the boys lost.

Or at least that's *one* way of looking at it.

Michael had been born with what's commonly known as fetal alcohol syndrome, which basically means his mom had abused so much liquor during her pregnancy, she may as well have been feeding him Jack Daniels through a baby bottle. Not exactly what a young, developing brain stem and body system need for optimal health. And it cost him. He ended up being saddled with some noticeable mental impairments that slowed down the way he processed information. He wasn't retarded, by any means, but let's just say he didn't challenge for valedictorian. School was a struggle. College wasn't likely in his future.

But *hope* was still in it because I'm not so sure he really lost out when he showed up here as the cast-off cargo from his father's shipwreck. What he received from his family and friends at the Ranch did more to light a fire of confidence inside him than all the nasty cigarette burns of his childhood had done in trying to snuff it all out, pressed like a hot coal against his bare flesh by a pair of abusive parents. He and Brodie, I was always glad to see, had become best buds almost from the start. They worked at the barn together. Showed horses together. When Brodie and Kelli were married, Michael was part of their wedding party.

So even though he didn't have everything he needed to go hit the books for four years at Alabama or Auburn, he did have the confidence to follow his skills and desires toward learning a trade. Industrial welding. Got pretty good at it too. And today, when he's not in Arkansas or Mississippi someplace, working an extended job as his own general contractor, he's back here at home, driving around in a $50,000 truck, and making more money every year than a lot of other kids (and college grads) ever will, even some of the ones he grew up with.

Financial success, of course, is not what makes him successful. I hope I've clearly established that point. What matters is that instead of seeing himself as a loser—somebody who came from nothing and had nowhere else to go—he trusted that everything he needed was truly inside himself somewhere and would keep on finding its way to a good, productive place.

The same is true for you.

Life, to a lot of people, seems like too steep of a hill to climb. Too many factors are working against you. Too many goals are beyond your reach. Too many of your competitors, you think, are already way out ahead of you, vying for the same piece of the pie—people who are more capable, more experienced, more confident in themselves, better connected, better credentialed. But the part of all this party pooping that does the most damage to your future is not typically a lack in your capabilities. Rather, it's the added drag of unwarranted worry, jealousy, inferiority, fear—an audio track that runs like a continuous loop of discouragement in your head, beating down your best attempts at healthy ambition, blacking out your sense of vision and forward thinking.

Defeating you before you even get on the field.

Unsurprisingly, then, that's how a lot of dreams end up dying on the vine, long before they've had a fighting chance to take any kind of fruitful shape. A pessimistic outlook can cloud all hopes of progress. Aversion to change and to the unknown complexities of life can scare you away from pursuing creative ideas for solving your problems. Unwillingness to ask for help or to ask questions limits your available options and opportunities as well as the ability to see yourself as serving a larger purpose than just validating your own worth as an individual.

The simple difference, in many cases, between success and failure is straight-up confidence. Trust. Belief. Assurance that no roadblock in your path is stubborn or insurmountable enough to keep you separated from what God has birthed in you or from wherever He wants you to go.

And that's what I see when I think about a guy like Michael—two things, really. I see fresh confidence growing like

Forty Years at Big Oak Ranch
First Decade (1974–1983)

Second Decade (1984–1993)

Third Decade (1994–2003)

On June 30, 1995 John Croyle had the honor of serving as one of the Olympic Torch Bearers.

Fourth Decade (2004–now)

Boys' Ranch (Established 1974)

Girls' Ranch (Established 1988)

John and Tee Croyle

Reagan's family:
John David, Reagan,
Cade, Will, and
Gibbs Phillips

Brodie's family:
Brodie, Kelli,
Sawyer, and
Luke Croyle

All of John and Tee's grandsons.

The whole family.

crazy in an unlikely place, and I see certain people who made it their own joyful mission to help put that confidence there.

Oh, and something else. I see you reaching new heights by becoming a good example of both: a confident liver and a confidence giver.

Confidence in God

I was groomed to be a ballplayer. My mom, to be honest, after the death of my sister, would just as soon I stayed indoors and played with Matchbox cars. She didn't want me even climbing trees, much less going full contact against live action on the local athletic fields. But between my dad's encouragement and my own love of sports, I knew what I was wired to do. Coming out of high school, I had received interest from UCLA to play basketball and from the University of Alabama to play football, among others. How do you lose, making that choice? This was going to be great.

Funny thing, though. God was using all that stuff to give me a launching pad, not a landing strip. And when I found myself bypassing the logical progression into pro football, I found myself staring instead at 120 acres of available land that its owner wanted a $50,000 down payment on—and not knowing what to do. I knew how to shed a fullback and a pulling guard and still get my hands on the ball carrier, but I sure didn't know how to pick his pocket of $50,000 while I was taking him to the ground. This new challenge was out of my league.

Especially on terms like these: "I don't want this to be no blankety-blank home for delinquents." That's what the seller had told me at our first meeting, as we discussed what he was asking for his property. "But if you want to keep this negotiation open, you've got forty-eight hours to raise the money. And five thousand of it I need today as earnest money."

I didn't have much going for me at the time, fiscally speaking. I didn't have fifty thousand of anything. But I did have trust—trust that God had led me into this whole thing to begin with and that He wouldn't leave me high and dry and flat on my face in failure. Even if this one particular opportunity for land didn't materialize, He was certain to work something out . . . someway.

It's really just that simple, I think. *We're* the ones who get scared and make it complicated. If I've learned anything in all these years, this one defining principle is at or near the top of that list: *the simplicity of God.* He says, basically, "Here's what I want you to do. If you do it, I'll bless you. I'll provide for you. But if you don't do it—if you run from it, if you think your way is better, if you disobey Me by chasing your own dreams instead—I'll need to correct you for your own good, which won't be a lot of fun for either one of us," so *you* decide. And let's see if you're smart enough to figure out which one is better: blessings or backtracking.

Duh-uh.

As somebody who's put himself in both positions, multiple times in my life, I can readily attest: trusting God is a whole lot more preferable to doubting Him, to shortchanging Him. He proved to me early on, "Look, son, you can trust Me. Don't even worry about it." The simplicity of God. Why do we feel such a need to make it any harder than that?

I've told some of the following narrative in other venues before, about what God did to enable me to seal the deal on that property. Let's start with the choice I made that day when the owner of the land laid out the overwhelming details of the sale. I went to my car alone and simply told God, "I'm willing." That's really all He wanted to hear. But just to show you again the variety of places He can pull blessings from, come follow along with me and try keeping up with the number of faith builders He manufactured for this flat-broke, unemployed children's home director without a child or a home to call his own.

For starters, the town of Gadsden, Alabama, had recently held a John Croyle Day (must've been a slow week for the city council), and they'd given me $5,000 as a . . . I don't know, a tax write-off or something. Truth is, the two men who were leaders of the University of Alabama alumni association (Rowan Vaughn and J. D. Johns) had wanted to give me a car. But when I told them, "I appreciate it, men, but what I really need is money to start getting this ranch built for kids," they'd given me the cash equivalent instead—and subsequently I'd won two dear friends for life. The $5,000 was exactly what I needed for earnest money to keep my contract deliberations ongoing.

There's one.

I had also been teaching a little Bible study for teenagers the past two or three years at the spacious home of Dr. William Buck. Every Saturday night in the off-season—winter and spring—as many as 150–200 kids would show up, and I'd think of something to say to them. None of it except the Bible reading part was probably worth remembering, but it was a good way to get a bunch of high schoolers off the street and in a wholesome environment on a weekend night, and we'll hope the Lord did some good with it while it lasted. But when this property negotiation with the forty-eight-hour time window came around, I went to Dr. Buck and asked if he might be willing to front me some money. Without batting an eye, he said he'd be happy to loan me $15,000—knowing all the time he'd never consider letting me pay it back to him.

That was $20,000 of what I needed.

Getting the rest, however, was even more remarkable than how the first part had come together.

I was out running a couple of errands near the little town of Boaz and bumped into the wife of one of my former teammates, big offensive lineman John Hannah, who had just been drafted by the New England Patriots. She told me, while we briefly chatted, that he was leaving for training camp in Massachusetts the next day, and asked, "Why don't you come up to the house and see him before he goes?"

OK. I mean, it wasn't like John and I were the best of friends or anything. We'd played ball together, been part of some great Alabama teams. But on weekends in Tuscaloosa, we ran with a different group of friends and teammates. So it wasn't the most routine of requests for his wife to invite me over like that, as if one of the items on his to-do list before leaving town was to be sure and see John Croyle.

But I was glad for the chance to stop by and wish him well.

"Come in here," he said. "Whatcha doing?"

We sat down at the kitchen table and begin to talk.

"Oh, you know, I'm getting ready to build that home for kids I've been talking about."

"Yeah, that's great."

But instead of just talking, John chose to get involved. And as rash as his promise seemed to me at the time (and probably should've sounded to him, as well), he never balked at it. That's just the kind of guy he is. He said to me, "Tell you what—whatever the Patriots give me for a signing bonus when I get my contract done, I'll give it to you. All of it. Whatever it is."

Turned out, of course, to be (you guessed it)—$30,000—the balance on what the seller of the land wanted me to pay him. At a conservative estimate that amount of money in 1974 would be more like five times as much today. $150,000 or more. Huge. And while it was a big enough blessing to forever make me indebted to John Hannah for investing in kids that neither he nor I even knew about yet, it was more importantly Exhibit C in a growing laundry list of examples that showed me God's amazing faithfulness. And the evidence has only continued to pile up around us as the years have trailed along.

I came into this thing with absolutely no reason, purely from a business moxie standpoint, to believe that I could raise or generate such a sizable amount of money with no tangible means of earning it.

But I did have confidence. Confidence in God. Trusted that I had what I needed.

And thanks to Him, did I ever. And He's never let me down.

Confidence to Burn

Like I said, though—trusting God to give you what you need as you follow Him each day is only part of what makes life such a rewarding adventure. It's only one facet of *who you are.* The other side of this equation is the privilege and responsibility of instilling confidence in other people.

Folks who don't have "it"—those who are more worried about building their own little kingdom, whose affinity for masking their flaws means routinely belittling other people in order to make themselves appear more capable and competent by comparison—will never enjoy the blessings of watching others succeed around them.

Coach Bryant, for example, at one time in his career at Alabama, had forty-two former players or assistant coaches who were head coaches in the NFL or college. Pretty strong! He knew what it meant to invest in people. He knew that no one, no matter how awesome they are, is ever able to achieve as much by themselves as they can accomplish together with others. They'll use up a lot of time and talent without ever seeing it turned loose into something that's truly worth celebrating.

My high school basketball coach, John Bostick, was another man who had "it." When he spoke, you hung on every word. You *stared* at him to keep from missing anything he said, in case you might miss a nuance or inflection by not both seeing *and* hearing him at the same time. He went on to coach basketball for C. M. Newton and Wimp Sanderson at Alabama, as well as for Coach Newton again in a later tenure at Vanderbilt. But in the years when he was head coach at Gadsden High, when I was there, he already knew how to make his guys want to run through a wall for him. There's nothing I wouldn't have done for that man. And every one of us felt the same way. He gave us confidence in ourselves and in what we could do. He established a mind-set inside of us that made us feel capable of taking down anybody we played. Anybody.

My junior year—his last—we went to the state finals. Lost to a team in the championship game that was far better than we were. Could outjump us. Could outshoot us. Could fake us right out of our jockstraps. But for three and a half quarters, we stuck with them stride for stride—because we knew we could. We *knew* it.

The way I saw it, every ball that came off the rim or the backboard was mine. The whole lane—it was mine. Anybody who dared to challenge me was simply in my way. Back off. Coach Bostick sent us into that game with confidence running out of our noses. So even though we lost, we didn't really lose that night. We excelled. Far beyond ourselves. For him.

My son Brodie remembers seeing that same kind of confidence exchange the first time he witnessed Tom Brady in action for New England. Even as the starting quarterback for the opposing Kansas City Chiefs, Brodie said you could feel the whole Patriots team rise up when Brady stepped under center. "When he walked on the field," he told me, "you knew he was there." The whole atmosphere, throughout the entire stadium really, just throbbed with new energy. Confidence. Everybody on that side of the ball rocked with confidence, merely by his presence and how he brought out the best in his teammates.

That was the game, you may recall—opening weekend, 2008—when Brady tore his ACL and was lost for the season, ending a streak of 111 consecutive starts that placed him fourth on the all-time list for NFL quarterbacks. But you can bet the Patriots' defensive unit dialed up Brodie in their sights from then on. And before it was over, they'd knocked him out of the game as well, shutting him down for the afternoon with a bruised shoulder. *That's for you, Tom Brady.*

That's what confidence will do.

Make you go to war, fight, break things.

Brodie's coach for most of his career there in Kansas City—Herm Edwards, now an ESPN studio analyst—is another guy who has "it." Brodie recalls his first team meeting as a rookie, expecting to find the NFL to be all business, all football, all the time. But the theme Coach Edwards employed at that opening session of the season, even amid the fire pit of win-now expectations, was more along the lines of: "I don't care nearly so much about you as a football player as I do about you as a man. Because if y'all are good husbands and good fathers—good men—the football part will take care of itself. I want guys of high character, high quality, not the ones who are just worried about making a dollar."

Just show me where to line up, Coach.

I'm ready to go to work for you.

John Wooden also—the "Wizard of Westwood"—famed basketball coach at UCLA for all those incredible runs of NCAA championships, was another person who had "it." Don't think I didn't wonder sometimes what it might've been like to play for him, alongside the likes of Lew Alcindor (aka Kareem Abdul-Jabbar) and others. I do know what it felt like to get personal letters from Coach Wooden, recruiting me to come play there. I can only imagine what suiting up for him would've been like.

If you're old enough to remember him, you recall he looked nothing like an upper-division college basketball coach, much less the best of all time. Instead, he had all the physical makeup and mannerisms of a chalk-stained calculus professor or biology teacher. Just to look at him, he didn't appear the kind of man who could get twenty-year-old athletes too worked up and excited about anything. But do you recall when his star center, Bill Walton, refused to cut his hair one year, in violation of Wooden's well-defined code against facial whiskers and unkempt appearance?

What could the coach really do about it, given the circumstances? What kind of falloff in performance could he risk running, just for failing to bend and change with the times, not letting premier players express themselves in something besides 1950s suit-and-tie decorum? And yet, when challenged by this outspoken national Player of the Year, when told he had no right to tell a grown man how to wear his hair, the coach said, "No, Bill, I guess I don't have the right to tell you how to wear your hair. But I do have the right to decide who's going to play. And . . .

"We're sure going to miss you."

Within twenty minutes the big redhead had rushed to the barber shop, flung his seven-foot body into the chair, and demanded a buzz cut—quick!—shaving his own face at the same time with a plastic razor and a cup of warm water in his lap.

A guy with principle like John Wooden, a guy with guts, a guy who's not afraid to tell people what they most need to hear—he'll always grow a deeper brand of confidence in his team than those men who never stop selling out for popularity.

Confidence. Are you giving it to people?

To your spouse? To your kids? To your employees? To your friends? To your pastor? To your coworkers? To anybody who looks to you for anything? Do you try to help inflame what you see in them and inspire them to confidence?

And what they may not receive as confidence in themselves, are you at least giving them confidence in *you*?

One of the greatest nights of the year around here is graduation. All of our kids go to Westbrook Christian, a K–12 school we operate for the community at large (like any private school) but also with the purpose of ensuring a quality, comprehensive education for our own children. So graduation is a big deal for the whole Ranch family. Yet it's also an open door each year to some characters from our kids' past who sometimes show up on the big night with intentions we can only guess at and try to prepare for.

This past year, for example, three of the girls came running up to me before the ceremony, frightened because they'd spotted their father in the parking lot, gathering with the rest of the audience, looking for them. I won't go into what I knew this man had done to his children. And I couldn't outright deny him the right to see his daughter receive her diploma. But I knew I needed to be watching him from my place on the platform and also to be aware of him and his presence afterward. I'd already alerted another friend, telling him, "If something happens, I'm going to holler for you."

But in that moment when those kids came rushing over, visibly shaken, they knew from long experience that they were safe with me, like with all the men at the Ranch. The confidence they felt—it's the same confidence I've seen in dozens, in hundreds of their faces whenever I've made the four promises we give to all our kids at Big Oak. They soak it up. They sense the stability and security. They know they're being listened to and watched over and cared for.

It means a lot.

It exudes confidence.

And you know what else? It just feels good. Being able to be counted on . . . being somebody they can trust . . . being sure that what you tell them is exactly what you're going to do.

That's what sends the confidence slinging in all directions. Toward *them*. Toward *you*. And toward God, of course, who's the only reason any of us should walk in any confidence at all. In the end everyone benefits when trust is embraced by others and embodied in ourselves. That's how everyone realizes they've got what they need.

Abundance

I don't know where these pages are catching you today. You may not be sporting a lot of confidence right now in yourself and in God's purpose for you. Perhaps you've taken some rough knocks in recent days and years, some from others' mistreatment or misjudgment of you, some from your own self-inflicted behavior or attitudes. Either way—from whatever source or combination of sources—your confidence is at a low ebb. So trusting in God is not something that's been coming easy for you. And from where you stand, you feel like you've got the evidence (or lack thereof) to prove it, to support your position.

But God has created the human heart—the human soul— with an endless capacity to grow and develop, a bottomless reservoir for receiving the plenty He can provide. That's why when you had your first son or daughter, and you couldn't believe how much you could actually love another human being—even *that* amount of love wasn't the limit on how much could be contained inside your heart. Know how I know? Because maybe, like a lot of us, you had a second son or daughter. And before you knew it, your love had grown to encompass *two* little people. You weren't confined to splitting up your love among the both of them, breaking it in half to make sure it could go around. Instead your love became even fuller and wider than before. It grew larger to meet the need and opportunity of the moment.

Some people, of course, have five or six kids, and their love grows to fill the whole family. A few people, like Tee and me and the other staff members here at the Ranch, have more than a hundred kids in our care at any one time. Not to mention the nearly two thousand children who have called Big Oak home since 1974. And it's no lie for me to say I'm crazy about all of them, every single one of them. Not because I'm Santa Claus (he's much shorter and fatter than I am), but because God gives me what I need. He gives us *all* what we need.

He has given and is giving to *you* what you need.

You can go to the bank on that.

Search the Bible, and you'll see that *abundance* is one of those words that appears all the way through it. Abundant joy, abundant goodness, abundant riches, abundant harvest, abundant supply, abundant peace, abundant love, abundant life. And one of the beauties of being a son of the King is realizing we've inherited, by the good pleasure of His grace, unlimited access to this unlimited storehouse of blessing. So the next time you get to worrying that you're going to be short on what you need for pursuing God's plans for your life, take it from a guy who's had two thousand kids. It's always safe to trust the Lord.

There's more room in your heart for His provision than you think.

Trust Him to fill it with everything you need.

CHAPTER 7

Choose

You're Creating a Lifestyle

 Life doesn't just happen.
Who you are is what happens.

So even though you can't choose where you're born or who you're born to, and even though various subsets of your life do involve other people's actions and random events and genetic health conditions you didn't directly initiate—still, the fact remains, you and I are largely the sum of our individual choices. Maybe not all $100 worth, but pretty near $97.50. When we cash in at the end of the day, we're piling up a stack that's primarily comprised of what we brought to the table ourselves and what we chose to do with it. Fair enough?

Agree with that?

Oh, some will beg to differ, of course—those who feel most of the choices they make in life have basically already been made for them. Not their fault, they say. Out of their control. Just playing the hand that's been dealt to them. Reading from the script. But from my experience and from what the Bible clearly demonstrates, each of us ultimately stands on our own two feet. And we must answer for how squarely we put our weight down on them. For how far and how straight we walked.

No, not everyone starts out at the same place, or even at a *good* place. Our kids at the Ranch are certainly proof of that. Maybe you are too.

And no, not all of us are tasked with ending up at the same place either. Life is not a game. We're not competing against other people or trying to outscore them with our performance. Truth is, God knows things about every one of us that should rightly keep us on the bench and out of commission for a long, long time. But His desire is to show just how amazing a job He can do in transforming all this mess of sin and sadness and the two-strike count against us into a lifestyle that consistently hits line drives and long balls and helps others come around to score.

That's true of *you*, just as it's true of *me*.

We all need His help. We all need a hand, a boost, a leg up.

But none of us is going anywhere—even with all God's power churning behind us—until we *choose* to cooperate with His sense of direction and purpose. That's why it's fair to say, looking at it from that perspective, that we determine who we become. We *choose* it . . . one choice after another, one choice at a time.

And from what I've noticed through the years, these choices generally congregate around three or four main hubs, areas where you can logically expect to be challenged pretty much every day. And by the time this collection of days has turned into a year, into a decade, into something approaching a lifetime, the downdraft—or if we're wise, the uplift—from the pattern of choices we've made will ripple beyond us into coming generations.

So this matters. It sets big things in motion. And even though some of these categories of choices we'll talk about may not seem like much to look at—fairly familiar, kind of what you expected—remember this: most of the mistakes we make are in places that seem incredibly obvious when we think back on them. So why don't we all just slow down here for a minute, long enough to think about these things ahead of time? Then instead of being shocked by how sensible and clear our lives look in hindsight—based on the choices we *should* have made—we can be amazed instead at how simple and uncomplicated some of the choices appear that are on our plate today.

We'll start, I think, with . . .

Moral Choices

The reason I love reading about the prodigal son in Jesus' famous parable is because I've *been* one . . . and *am* one . . . and I'm capable of being one again before I leave the house for work this morning. So the idea of knowing that a guy like him "came to his senses" in a pigpen in the middle of nowhere (Luke 15:17) gives me hope that I can run home to my heavenly Father at any time after failing Him and expect to be received with the same kind of celebration and forgiveness.

But what I really need to hear and be inspired by, equally as much (or more), is what Daniel did in Babylon, when he was being coaxed into embracing a pagan lifestyle—one that differed from his Hebrew upbringing not only in look and feel but in overall purpose and rationale. Instead of taking the path of least resistance, instead of justifying the gray areas, instead of leaving himself the accommodating backdoor of "coming to his senses" later on, the Bible says he "made up his mind" not to defile himself with the king's food and drink, not to change himself so he could better adapt to a culture of compromise (Dan. 1:8 NASB). He "resolved" (NIV), he "determined" (HCSB), he "purposed in his heart" (KJV)—pick your translation, but you get the point. He *chose* not to give in, even when presented with a decadent, luxurious, appetizing menu of lifestyle considerations. He led out with his right mind rather than just hoping to return to it later.

And we know from what we read of his story in Scripture that the legacy that flowed from his wise, disciplined outlook resulted in great achievement, great usefulness, great influence, and great faith—so great that he didn't even wig out at the prospect of a *lions' den* as part of the cost of doing God's business.

Thankfully, God's willingness to forgive us, like we've seen and like we know, is a blessed component of His relationship program. Without it we'd all be dead. No hope, no way. So the frequent repenting of our sins is therefore an imperative of life for imperfect people like you and me. Being able to seek and receive restoration is something we should all be wholly grateful for and well practiced in.

But holy cow, aren't you just about sick of making the same stupid mistakes, over and over again? Of staying hooked up to the remorse and regret machine? Of constantly needing to sleep off the aftereffects of another screw-up? Can you imagine how tremendous it would feel to string together a few straight weeks of confidence-building character and not need to learn the hard way what comes instead from being so selfish and quick tempered? Again?

I know. That's what I thought.

So I'll use the example here that just sails immediately to mind, especially for men when we start grappling with our moral integrity: every man's battle, the allure of sexual lust. And here's what I'd say about that, based on what I've seen in myself, based on how it relates to setting an example for the young men we parent here at the Ranch, and based on what I say all the time whenever I speak to men's groups. "Guys! Your children are watching you. I swear they don't notice the woman walking by you nearly as much as they notice her reflection in *your eyes*."

So when you're fighting that urge to stare or to sneak a second or third look, turn that fight into a fight for your son's lifetime of freedom and self-control in this matter, letting him learn from your strong show of manly restraint. Turn it into a fight for your daughter's self-esteem and self-worth, knowing her father isn't a lecher who prizes physical attractiveness above all, but rather a man of honor who upholds her dignity, loves her with pure devotion, and affirms what's truly of value in her as a young woman . . . because it shows in your example of how you treat other women in public.

If you see enough beer commercials and sitcoms, the pattern becomes ridiculously, shamefully obvious. Living with runaway lustful thoughts and desires groups you into a blanket stereotype that makes you *exactly* like everybody else. It really doesn't take much of a man, does it, to be like that—to ogle women on the street or from across the parking lot, to nearly topple over a fern planter in the shopping mall while you're weaving your way past the Victoria's Secret store window.

But to turn away and say: "Lord, help me. I don't want to be led along into sin like this—like some mindless, knuckle-dragging Neanderthal. I don't want to get my jollies from every low-cut top or miniskirt that bounces by, instead of being true to my wife in my heart and mind"—that's what I call putting the *more* in your *morality*. That's making a choice that will change your life.

I mean, there just comes a time when you need to say, "I'm not going to be like everybody else anymore." OK? Am I right?

And what goes for this one particular temptation, you can spread out across whatever other lingering issues keep tripping you up—pride, laziness, anger, rudeness, worry, bitterness, idolatries, addictions. Fill in the blank. And while I know the easiest course is just to let it ride, not obsess over it, figure you probably deserve it after everything you've gone through, I think you know the better choice—the winning choice—you might even say the *obvious* choice—is to do what you know to be right. Isn't it?

I mean, isn't it?

Obvious?

To be pure minded? To be patient? To be humble? To be honest?

So let's quit coddling ourselves with excuses for why something feels good, feels right, feels safer, feels allowable under the circumstances. Let's talk instead about what it means when *who you are* is by and large a person that you, your spouse, and your kids could really look up to. And let's wonder what might happen if we courageously made the kind of daily, moral decisions that show them how it's done.

Because remember, with every choice, you're creating a lifestyle.

Family Priorities

My dad was a hard worker. One of the more tireless men I've ever known. My mom held down a day job while also taking care of the house and all the other stuff mothers do. She did it. Just about every adult I can recall, growing up, seemed like they put in a full week's effort and didn't back away from any of their responsibilities. In general, what I saw were diligent, industrious, no-nonsense, hardworking people.

And yet I don't think they hardly *ever* felt what people feel today—this (what would you call it?)—this unrelenting sense of running behind, where home and family are constantly getting the last of our energy . . . if any. I don't ever remember feeling slighted by my parents, like they were way too busy for me— like I was a problem, a nuisance, a burden, third or fourth on the list of what mattered to them that day.

When did this start?

I mean, I know not all the parents of my childhood generation put a lot of effort into their roles at home. The nostalgic, white-picket-fence family of yesteryear wasn't ever quite as pristine and well ordered in real life as it seems when you look back at the Polaroids. And of course, from meeting the kids who've come to live with us through the years, I know more of the things that were happening behind closed doors than most of us can imagine.

But I'm just saying—all this computer technology that was supposed to make our lives so much simpler and free us up to kick back at the end of the day and roast hot dogs with the kids at sundown—I'm sorry, I don't see that happening. What I see are people running a hundred miles an hour, tethered to their handheld devices, answering work e-mails from 9:30 to 11:00 at night, and basically telling their families just to take a backseat because of what their job and life demands.

And I don't know how mothers and fathers are supposed to exert much influence on their children if they barely, if ever, give them their undivided attention, if their heads are stuffed so constantly full of work and meeting notes and deadlines and phone calls and tomorrow's to-do list that they scarf down what little time is left over to spend with their kids in a feverish attempt to get back to business or just to get back to whatever interests them more.

We've got a lot of absentee parents these days. And a lot of them are living right there in the house with their kids.

Daddy?

"Just a minute, baby."

Daddy?

"I said just a minute."

Daddy?

"Would you shut up and wait?"

Daddy?

"I'm busy! Go ask your mother."

Sure, I know why it happens. Maybe the man's a doctor or surgeon, and it takes him a long time to come down from the patients and procedures he's been forced to handle in a day. Maybe the man's a weekend musician or filmmaker, and his work buddies are on his back to come over and get busy on whatever project he's slowing them down on. Maybe he's short of his sales quota this month, and he's working a complicated deal that he badly needs to pull off, but he's doing it with a client who expects and demands almost 24/7 access and attention. Or—heaven help us—maybe he's a preacher who's so busy out there serving the spiritual needs and hand-holding expectations of his congregation that he's neglecting his wife and the only two or three people in the world who call him Daddy.

I tell pastors whenever I get a chance to speak to them: "Let's get this right, gentlemen. I'm not a preacher, but I know what it's like to have a lot of people needing you and counting on you to listen and be there for them. And some of you are telling the world how to save their families from wolves while your own family back home is being attacked by wolves every day, and you're not there to protect them. Everybody *else* is learning how to live and cope and be victorious in life because of your tireless ministry, but what about the people you're primarily responsible for leading and loving and equipping in life?"

Easy guilt trip to lay on them? I guess so. But they know it's true if that's what's happening (or not happening) in their homes. And it's why a lot of pastors' kids end up hating church, hating church people—*hating God*—for always seeming to be what kept their fathers from being what they needed them to be. Remember, God *never* calls us to sacrifice our families at the altar of ministry. *Never!*

I'm not meaning to blast away at preachers here. They get enough flak, even for the truly great things they do. But this is why I tell the folks on our staff all the time: "When you go home, drop your briefcase of files at the door, and don't think about it anymore. Don't think about the Ranch, the kids, the school—you just focus on your family. Then when you get ready to walk out the door next morning, pick up what you placed there the night before, go sit in your car, and get your head back into the groove of what's coming up that day. But not *until* then. Don't take it home. Don't ever take it past the door."

Because bottom line, it's a choice.

Oh, maybe not every day. Not in certain seasons of intensity when you're needed around the clock. But if this kind of out-of-balance obsession becomes more rule than exception, you're witnessing the lead-up to what will ultimately become a tragic situation. I'm not exaggerating. Make the choice to make your family more important to you than people who won't cry at your funeral.

Remember, you're creating your own lifestyle.

Get Some Rest

You can only imagine what the lives of our houseparents are like at the Ranch. They are truly the heroes of the Big Oak story. Most people who ask about what they do and how they function in our homes get hung up on the laundry-level aspects of it—supper for eight kids every night, helping everybody with their homework, getting them where they need to go, taking them to the doctor, the dentist, all that stuff. It's truly the all-American family schedule on steroids.

I guess, in another century or two, we could probably hire a robot to do a lot of that. But what our houseparents do, that no maid or dishwasher can do, is to *love* our children.

I put that word in italics, but what I should do is make it as big as this whole page, outline it in black, and color it with every shade in the crayon box. That's how much they love, *love*, *LOVE* our children. They love the you-know-what out of them, to get them to see heaven. Heaven is going to be full of our kids because of what God has done (and is doing) through these heroes of ours . . . and theirs.

I've seen them come in here to the office to meet a new boy or girl who's going to be part of their family and do nothing else for fifteen minutes but tell them how they can't wait to be their mama or daddy, how nothing harmful will ever be able to touch that child again, and how they will protect and care for them and love every second of having them in their family.

One of the kids who came here recently had endured so much crud from her parents and her abusive living situation, she was totally fed up on life—even more than most. Just didn't see much hope or point in it anymore. Hated herself. Felt like she was too far gone for anything good to happen to her, ever again. But after weeks and months of being inundated with unconditional love from her houseparents, being shown the grace of Christ on everyday display, she eventually reached the point where she could say, "I don't know what it is, but I want what you have. I didn't think anybody could ever make me feel lovable again, but now I do. And it's all because of you."

Ask Reagan, who works most closely with them every day, and she'll tell you without any hesitation: the bond between houseparent and child is the true, leading agent of change that the Holy Spirit uses to make our work happen the way it does. No doubt. Hands down.

Excuse me, though. I'm getting off subject a little—which is not hard to do when I start talking about our housemoms and dads and what they pull off for our kids around here. I could tell you a whole lot more, actually, and I'd still be leaving out 80 or 90 percent of it.

But my reason for bragging on them so much in this chapter, and telling you about the Herculean tasks they perform, is to say this to you: You can't do what these guys do without *rest*.

They could not be as awesome as they are if they're burning out their rings every day with no letup, never taking any time away to cool off and recapture. One of the reasons the retention rate of our houseparents is something like twenty or thirty times the national average is because we make sure they blow some fresh air into their lives. Anything less, and we'd be losing them right and left. And what's worse, we'd lose some of that connection and consistency that breaks the chains of abuse and chaos in our kids.

Our mission here, our life here at the Ranch, is all encompassing, all consuming. And yet I'm sure you could probably say the same thing about your life too. Each of us is capable, in our own way and in our own settings, of seriously overdoing it. And the consequences to our health, our relationships, our overall competence, and certainly our spiritual life will only compound in problems as long as we persist in trying to be superman or supermom.

Self-care is what we call what we expect of our houseparents. And we mean it.

We give them time off. We encourage them to find something—anything—that lets them take a deep breath through the day, through the week. Even if it's going for a walk or getting a workout, or slipping away to get a cup of coffee, moments and periods of rest are *musts* in their schedules.

What about you? Are you doing that?

If you're not—if you're not making that choice—you're doing it at a cost much higher than you can contemplate, even higher than your perception of yourself and your stamina and your ability to be everything to everybody all the time. No matter what other people are putting on you and no matter how codependent they make you feel, you won't be any good to anybody once you've flamed out and stuck a fork in it. Sure, finding time to take a break may always be a challenge, and it may keep giving you that guilty sense that you're being lazy and selfish.

But we're created by God to experience regular rhythms of rest. (Remember the Sabbath?)

So remember what *you're* creating whenever you do it.

You're creating a lifestyle.

Money Matters

So when you're dealing each day with temptations and moral issues, you've got *choices*. When you're making real-time determinations for what your priorities are going to be, you've got *choices*. When you're mapping out your schedule for the week, the month, or the foreseeable future, you may not think you're in much control over what goes in those blanks. But I'm telling you, you've still got some *choices*.

And while we're here, let me toss out one more for you: the whole subject of how you spend, handle, give, and approach your money.

You've got some *choices* to make there.

I can tell you for a known fact, at Big Oak Ranch, we're careful with where our money goes. And we hold ourselves inscrutably accountable for every dime and dollar we receive. Not that others don't, but here we sure do.

Listen, I might make mistakes. I have. And will. But we've made the choice that we will *never* mess with our integrity in how we handle the funds people entrust to us.

A guy may hand me an envelope—as someone did, just two or three weeks ago—with several thousand dollars in it, cash, and tell me to do whatever I want to do with it. Well . . . I mean, how easy would it be? Take a little off the top? Deposit what's left? No. Never crossed my mind. I asked that gentleman to come to the office, brought him upstairs to meet our business manager, had him watch me hand over the money, and then we printed him out a receipt under our letterhead for the full amount.

I've never used anybody or anybody's money for personal gain. I never will. I've made that choice. And I'll never underestimate the sacrifice that's involved when people give to us.

If any one event really sealed this attitude forever in me, as far as feeling enormously accountable for the money we receive, it was a gift that came into the office one day, many years ago, with a simple letter attached to it. A big donation. $53,000. From a guy in Seattle who said he'd read about us in *Reader's Digest* and decided he wanted to help our kids. "I just really liked the story," he said.

Well, if he'd felt prompted to give us more than $50,000, based on what little he knew of the Ranch from an article he picked up, what might he give us, I thought, if he knew the whole story?

So guess what I did? Booked a flight to Seattle, packed one of our nice, wool, leather-sleeved, Big Oak jackets in my suitcase, and decided to go give this guy some one-on-one time, wanting to flesh out some of the stories I could tell him about our children and our children's home.

Once I touched down and folded into my rental car, I drove toward the section of town indicated by the street address I'd been given and the map I was using. But something didn't look right. I remember calling my secretary from the car to see if I'd written down these numbers correctly.

"Yes," she said, repeating the information back to me. "Sounds right."

Then why was I in what looked like the lower end of town, with the nose of my car pulled up to a house that appeared to have been converted into a quadruplex? Rough. Rundown. Hmm.

So I wasn't sure what to expect when I crawled out of the car and ventured toward one of the first-floor apartments. But I knew I was in the right place when the guy who opened the door said, "John. Thank you for coming."

He invited me in. And once inside, I did what anybody would do—gave a quick glance around. All the furniture was of Goodwill caliber or worse, well worn, ripped in a few places. The kitchen, visible from the front entry, was no more than four feet across at its widest dimension, with a couple of little college-dorm hot plates situated where the cooktop should've been, a small fridge and several darkened shelves, not even any cabinets. For wall art a Big Oak Ranch calendar was hanging on a nail nearby.

"I know you'd probably like to take me to lunch," he said, "but if it's OK, could we just eat here? Just visit and talk?"

"Uh, sure," I said. "I'd be honored."

So we talked while he opened the lid on a can of tomato soup, added some water to it, cut up a few carrots and celery sticks to drop in. He then took out two tea bags, added water to another saucepan, and left it to simmer. Then he shuffled over to where I was seated. Sat down across from me. "Now let's visit."

OK, so I'm sure you know where I'm going with this. He obviously, from all appearances, wasn't a multimillionaire who could easily peel off $50,000 from his personal account and never miss it. On the contrary, according to the story he told me about where the money had come from, he had hopped a freight train down from Alaska to Seattle, and somehow got word in a hobo camp that a couple of his aunts had died in San Francisco and had left him a sizable amount of money. When he found out how much it was—$53,000—he told me the Lord spoke to his heart, and said, "Why don't you give it to those kids?"

I'm serious.

He went on to tell me a lot more stuff like that—about how he had once worked in Silicon Valley, about some unfortunate events that had occurred in his life, about how he'd built a pipe bomb to retaliate against two men who'd mugged him, but the explosives had gone off prematurely and left him needing an artificial implant in one eye—yet how not long after his hospital stay, he'd been able to find work as a handyman, and how the Lord had given him his "wonderful home."

By this point I was ready to crawl under the floor, realizing what my initial motive for going out there had been and how drastically different I'd found the situation to be. Nearly speechless with shame over my motives, I said to him finally: "I came out here to say thank you, sir. I had no idea about your life or why you'd given us the money. But it means the world to me. And I do hope you'll accept a little gift from me, from us." I pulled the coat from my bag and handed it to him. "Oh!" he said, overjoyed, as if I'd just presented him with a pair of cruise tickets.

He hopped up, slid the jacket on, held out his arms, eyeing the fit. "Thank you, thank you," he said. "This is wonderful. I didn't have one."

A coat.

Didn't have one.

In Seattle.

I remember two things distinctly from the remainder of that afternoon. I remember getting back in my car, releasing a guilty sigh, closing my eyes toward heaven, and saying, "God, *please*, forgive me. And don't ever let me forget the way I'm feeling right now." I also remember being at the Seattle airport waiting for my return flight to depart, scanning the shelves for a big sleeve of cashews, my favorite snack, at one of those overpriced stores in the terminal. Eighteen dollars, the label said—a price I might not ordinarily have flinched at, given the location of the shop. You know, it's like movie popcorn. Captive audience. They can charge whatever they want.

But that was the day I quit buying expensive bags of cashews at airport stands, like I'd always obliged myself before. It was also the day I vowed before God that even if I failed to pass certain tests of leadership in the future, I would never fail Him when it comes to handling our finances with total, complete integrity. I will never abuse the trust placed in us by those who freely share their resources with us.

I don't care what kind of role you play in life, now or in the days to come—you will invariably encounter situations where your integrity and wisdom and stewardship with money will be challenged. But trust me, no financial temptation is too small not to err on the side of full transparency and accountability. And no financial temptation is too large for a person who chooses ahead of time not to have their head turned by it.

It's a lifestyle decision.

Staying to the Pathway

You're not just making choices. You're creating a lifestyle. They all add up. And they all take you somewhere.

So whether you're seventeen and making decisions for what you're going to be doing this spring break, or you're in your thirties and sneaking off to indulge some unhealthy pleasure, or you're middle-aged and entertaining a business deal that's maybe not completely on the up-and-up, there's something a lot bigger happening here than the specific details of these one or two decisions. These choices are determining *who you are*. And once they're stacked end to end, they'll go a long way toward determining who you'll be in the future.

So choose carefully. And choose wisely. Because you're not just choosing for yourself. And you're not just choosing for the moment.

You're choosing your lifestyle.

CHAPTER 8

Multiply

You're Making a Difference

Never know what you're liable to see around here at the Ranch, just driving around. You might see kids in safety goggles edging the grass around their homes with a string trimmer. Housemoms loading the night's groceries into their twelve-passenger vans, backed up to our fully stocked warehouse where we store donated items. Two randomly even teams locking horns in a pickup basketball game, working to get open and clapping for a pass—while another little set of three or four boys stands off to the side, ready to take winners.

But I couldn't remember the last time I'd seen a pup tent pitched by the side of the lake, the little body of water that centers our property at the boy's ranch. Here it was, Friday afternoon, getting sort of late, and—who in the world had decided to camp out for the night?

Pulling a little closer, wheeling around the long driveway, I saw this short, kind of stumpy fellow emerge from the tent, followed by a little boy, maybe eight years old or so.

"Hey there," I called through the open truck window, trying to make out who it was.

"Oh, hi, Mr. John," the man answered, starting to walk toward me.

Once I heard his voice, saw his gait, I immediately knew who it was. Let's call him Nick. Fifteen or twenty years before, maybe longer, his JPO (juvenile probation officer) had brought him to us, saying he'd been caught stealing food and skipping school. They'd found him living alone with his brother and sister, his mom and dad having apparently abandoned them all. The younger two had been placed with the state's department of human resources, but the judge had wanted to see if we'd be willing to take custody of Nick ourselves. He was the oldest. Only twelve.

And look at him now . . . in his thirties, a fishing pole slung over his shoulder, traipsing toward me on the same path I'd seen him walk a hundred times as a kid. "I hope you don't mind," he said, as he drew closer. "There wasn't anybody here. We just wanted to come camp out."

"No problem," I said. "Who's that little fisherman you got with you?"

"Oh, this is my son," he said, proudly putting a hand along the boy's shoulder, then beaming back in my direction, showing him off. "I've been telling him about this place, but we haven't been able to get over here. I just wanted him to see where I grew up."

"Absolutely. Make yourself at home."

I guess they've been back ten or twelve times since then, just to hang out together, over here at his daddy's old stomping grounds. It's given me the chance to learn that Nick today is a deacon in his church, a teacher in youth Sunday school, and by all accounts a terrific husband and father.

But most of all, he's living proof to me that of all the things we could spend our time doing, of all the things we could accomplish with these few years we're given on the earth, none is more valuable than pouring ourselves into other people, investing in their success, accumulating portfolios of memories with others rather than amassing meaningless possessions for ourselves.

Are you doing that?

Investing in other people?

Now wait, before I lose you, I can already hear some of the objections firing up, the exemption clauses. "That's easy for *you* to say, John Croyle. Raising and rescuing children is your business. You've got nine-to-five every day to be doing nice things for people. You're able to wake up every morning focusing all your energies on those kids. Me—I've got to go to work today. I won't get home until suppertime tonight, and after that it'll be 8:00, and I'll be trying to get a few things done before going to bed and starting the whole thing back up again tomorrow. It's not that I'm being greedy or trying to ignore people or anything. I just don't have the time. Maybe on the weekends . . . maybe . . ."

OK, fine. We can go there if you want to. I realize not every shift at the factory or every staff meeting at the office lends itself to a feel-good story like Nick's or like some of the others I've been able to share in this book. (To tell you the truth now, it's not all Vacation Bible School around here either. There's a lot more involved in what we do than the part that shows up in the photos and feature articles for the monthly newsletter.) But when I talk about multiplying ourselves in others' lives, I'm not just talking about the highly involved commitment of adopting an orphan or paying for his education or providing for his care in hopes of seeing him turn out right. That's not the baseline I'm drawing, OK?

I'm saying investing in other people is an attitude.

It's a shift in who's center stage in your next conversation. It's the decision to make others the focus of your attention.

And I'll bet, if you go into the next day with your antenna redirected away from what *you* need, what *you* deserve, what *you* consider essential to functioning and feeling normal as a person, you'll notice (as I do) a lot of things that are entirely trained on yourself, your habits, your preferences, your stomach. And while those aren't necessarily *bad* things, you do at least need to realize up front, the payout they give is self-contained within that moment. They are rewards in themselves. And that's it. Once *Monday Night Football* is over, that's all you've got to show for it. Once you've drained the dregs on that fancy $3.95 cup of coffee you say you can't start the day without, the only thing it leaves behind is an extra bathroom stop at 10:30.

And even those things that make up the loyal, legitimate parts of your workday—when you really analyze them—can too often be focused primarily on how *you're* being received, whether people find *you* so charming and funny, who's noticing the good job *you're* doing, and if you're getting what *you* want from it all.

So the question, when you get right down to it, is whether you're going to spend most of your days just basically adding and subtracting from your own account, or if you'd rather be multiplying instead . . . through others.

I've been privileged to spend some time with a man named Jim Wilson Jr., an extremely successful builder and real estate developer, whose company created the Galleria shopping mall in Birmingham, among many other high-profile projects and enterprises. I've seen him on a job site—boss of the whole company—going up to gardeners, plumbers, heavy-equipment operators, saying, "How you doing? I'm Jim Wilson (like they didn't know). What's *your* name?"

He didn't need to do that. *He* didn't need those people. How many other mulch spreaders and concrete pourers could he have gone out and found or contracted for? These just happened to be the guys who'd been assigned to this job on this day. They would never expect a handshake and a few minutes with the top dog of the operation or feel slighted if they saw him walk past them without stopping to visit. A nod and a wave . . . tops.

After all, how many layers of hierarchy stood between Jim Wilson and whatever he felt like communicating to the hourly wage laborers his company was paying for? And yet he went in, went over, went out of his way to treat these workers with respect and dignity, to ask about their families, to see if they needed anything.

Impressive leadership.

But basically just a simple investment.

And you can bet those guys put their whole backs into whatever they were charged with completing for the rest of the day—just because a man cared enough to treat them like a person with value, not just a faceless form in a hard hat and work boots.

There's a reason the only multiplication tables we ever need to know are the ones that run up to just about ten or twelve . . . you know, four times two, seven times five, three times eight. Because from such simple math equations as these—the kind even a third-grader can figure out and memorize in his head—you can eventually end up with numbers so big, they won't fit on your calculator readout.

There are two kinds of people: those who can't even go fill up their gas tank or buy a newspaper without running into two or three people who consider them as friends; and those who couldn't come up with a short list right now of people who'd serve as their pallbearers. The difference between the two is not defined by any huge investments they've made (or not made) in others. The difference comes from a daily diet of small, ongoing investments that multiply over time into changed lives and encouraged hearts.

It's from traveling through each day with an others focus.

I remember hearing a call-in segment on a local radio station while I was out in the car one afternoon. The guest that day was Bart Starr. If that name doesn't ring a bell, you're either well under thirty years of age or you'd much rather spend your Sunday afternoons in the fall watching old movies on TV than the game of the week. Bart Starr played football at Alabama but more famously went on to be quarterback for Vince Lombardi's championship teams at Green Bay in the 1960s and also coached there for the Packers for nearly ten years after his playing career was over. A true NFL legend. Hall of Famer. So you can imagine the kinds of questions people might want to ask him while they had a crack at talking with him. Memories of playing in the Ice Bowl in 1967 against the Dallas Cowboys. Locker room stories and insights from the highly quotable Coach Lombardi. For anybody who enjoys old-time football history, it was a sports junkie's playground. I believe I ended up counting fourteen calls that came in during that one hour. I'm sure many more on hold didn't get through.

And not one of them was about football.

"Mr. Starr?"

"Please call me Bart."

"No—no, I could never do that. Mr. Starr, my wife was coming home one day in the pouring rain and had a flat tire. This Lexus pulled up next to her. Guy got out, took his coat off, asked her to pop the trunk. He changed her tire, tapped on the window—soaked to the skin—gave her a thumbs-up, and sent her on her way. She never told you, but she knew it was you. And I just called to say thank you, Mr. Starr."

One after another.

One times fourteen.

Got to want to get in on some of that action.

Home Investments

But don't hear me trying to turn this into a Hands Across America campaign. I mean, sure, part of the way this idea cashes out can be through, oh—let's say, running a 10k for diabetes research, or keeping bottles of water in your car to hand out to homeless men at a traffic stop, or randomly slipping quarters into people's parking meters. Stuff like that. The whole idea of seeing yourself and your resources—your money, your time, your talent, your kind words—as investments to make in others' lives can result in all sorts of creative, proactive moments and long-term commitments. And the more this mind-set becomes *who you are*, the more opportunities you'll spot and be ready to jump on.

Having said that, however, I want to steer this discussion in a direction that's a little more ordinary than where some of these activities are likely to take you. Yet it's a place where your return on investment is likely to be much, much greater and definitely of more personal interest.

I'll start by saying it this way: from where I sit, from the things I see, I'm happy just knowing that our kids at the Ranch are no longer being stolen from—their innocence, their future, their childhood. They're no longer being set up for abuse because of being mostly helpless to defend themselves against people who, by virtue of their position of authority, should've been caring for them and loving them and making them feel safe instead. And while I'm glad to know, of course, that you would never betray your son or daughter to such a heartless extent, I don't think you'll mind my asking: Is it possible that you're sometimes satisfied with just putting a roof over their heads, clothes on their backs, food on the table, and giving them a clean bed to sleep in? Have you considered whether you're truly multiplying the value of their relationship with you rather than just keeping them up, keeping things going?

Because as much pain as I've witnessed from watching kids deal with being orphans—their mom and dad both literally dead—I've found certain things to be almost worse, if you can imagine. *Emotional* orphans, whose parents pull back and withhold love from their children. *Mental* orphans, whose parents don't really try making a connection with their kids' interests, who don't take time to value their distinctiveness. *Spiritual* orphans, whose parents may be genuinely loving and engaged with them but not in a way that models or guides them toward a lifelong relationship with God.

And—again—while you would never sink to some of the wicked depths that I've seen these dynamics morph into among certain moms and dads, there are many different levels where some of these same conditions can still occur, even in less horrific form. It may not amount to a total depletion of the child's heart and identity, like we've often seen in our particular line of work, but it can end up transacting as slow, leaking withdrawals from their account. Subtractions. Minus signs.

I've seen firsthand the amount of difference that can take place when children are regularly and intentionally affirmed, when they're given room and opportunity to express themselves through discovering their own talents and interests, when they're led regularly into the Word and shown by parental example the ways of living correctly. It's enough to make me passionate about being sure that homes and families like yours are becoming healthy breeding grounds for this kind of growth.

Real multiplication.

I heard recently that the cost of raising a child these days—when you factor in their housing, food, health care, dental work, insurance, schoolbooks, sports, lessons, and all—is a whopping $240,000. If they go off to college, this amount can double to nearly $500,000. *Per child.* Just to get them up and out on their own.

That's a lot of money. A lot of hours at the plant. A lot of sales and savings and probably some side jobs to boot.

But I'm afraid a lot of parents are putting that enormous level of outlay into the children who share their milk jug and mailing address and yet aren't daily, devotedly, pragmatically occupied in working that investment for all it's worth. I still see too many of them who, despite loving their children dearly, still regard them in practical terms as drains and drags on their own personal likes, ambitions, and interests. And therefore, the children become more like a customary add-on to their parents' lives—cute when they do something funny or draw favorable attention to the family, but not always worth much more investment than what parents feel obligated to pay for.

I just like to think of these children as treasures. Jesus, you know, said not to "collect for yourselves treasures on earth, where moth and rust destroy and where thieves break in and steal. But collect for yourself treasures in heaven, where neither moth nor rust destroys, and where thieves don't break in and steal" (Matt. 6:19–20). And when we try to figure out what kind of things these "treasures in heaven" are likely to include, I don't think our minds need to go almost exclusively toward what we can do for the new neighbors who moved in across the street, for example, or the starving villagers of central Africa, or the friend whose wife has been diagnosed with cancer, or whatever occupies the agenda for another weeknight meeting at church. Good stuff to do? Absolutely. The more, the merrier.

But what about those treasures that are right there in the living room with you? What about those little ones you may try to get into bed early so you can catch your 9:00 television program? What about those precious kids who can multiply more from a single memory with you than you could possibly accrue by spending another weekend with your hunting buddies or scheduling another sensible but probably unnecessary business trip?

Treasures. Investments.

Which ones are you trying the hardest to multiply?

I mentioned earlier how my dad never failed to miss but a tiny, tiny percentage of my games as a longtime football and basketball player. Tee and I worked hard to do the same with our kids. We made sure our presence was known at Reagan's and Brodie's sporting events and other things. Even today, as grandparents, we tack up the lists of baseball and basketball schedules, make sure we know who's playing when. Sometimes we're even forced to split up in order to cover them all. She'll go to one; I'll go to the other one. But we never want our grandkids to say, "Memo and Poppy don't care. They don't even come to my games." Oh, yes we do. And they know it.

Yeah, it's just a simple example. A small investment. And I'm inclined to think, without even knowing you, that you're probably faithful in doing this kind of thing for your kids or grandkids as well. Right? Good for you. But in this way and a hundred other ways, we all just need to make sure our currency of choice comes from the investments we make in our children, in our family, as well as in others that God brings across our path or leads us to pursue—because they are worth every sacrifice, every available moment, and every contribution of our undivided attention. Our kids especially need to know that we will go to the wall for them, will do anything for them, in order to help maximize what God has already placed inside them.

That's just who we are . . . because we believe in who *they* are.

Five years ago a man came and interviewed with our staff, applying to be a houseparent. But he and his wife already had six children of their own, and we told him flat out his family size alone precluded him—by sheer logistics—from being able to serve in our ministry model and the types of homes we run for the kids.

So—rebuffed—he asked if he could apply instead to be director of the entire girls' ranch.

Hmmh. I laughed at that. I mean, I was actually serving in that position myself at the time and was admittedly doing a poor job of it. It was stretching me pretty thin, and I couldn't give it the amount of thought and oversight it rightly deserved. But the *nerve* of this guy, coming in here and deciding he was qualified to run the whole show, not having any background for it. When I had the chance to meet him myself, I actually told him to his face (I'm ashamed to say) that I thought he was a presumptuous jerk.

Not very nice, but that's how I felt.

"No, sir, I'm not a presumptuous jerk," he said, with noticeable poise, politely.

"Well, what *are* you then?"

"I'm chief of staff at West Point."

(Oh.)

And that wasn't all. He also served as athletic director, as well as being department head and professor of English there, and was in the process of rewriting the entire honor code for the Army. Nothing jerkish, presumptuous, or overstated at all in who he was and what he was offering. In addition, he had a fairly well-versed knowledge of the Ranch and its operation, having given to and supported us for quite a while.

OK. So with this new information as subtext, I pushed him through a number of additional interview sessions. Tee and I even went out to eat one night with him and his wife. Still weren't sure. I mean, this was a tall assignment we were talking about. And even with the broad shoulders of experience and trust this gentleman was carrying around, he needed to be thoroughly checked out and run through the paces.

But one thing became clear from our several long conversations—this environment was truly the kind of setting where he wanted to raise his own children. As much as he wanted to become part of the mission and message of Big Oak Ranch, he obviously viewed this job through the lens of his entire family.

Being able to come here, if possible, was a serious, deliberate, prayed-up intention on his and his wife's part.

Finally, during our third extended meeting late that summer, when he could maybe tell that I was warming up to the idea in general and to his candidacy in particular, he said to me, "By the way, if we did come here, I'd like to ask a favor."

"Sure, what's that?"

"If I were to retire from the Army today, I'd leave with the rank of lieutenant colonel. But if I could wait until December, I'd be able to retire as a *full* colonel, which would mean an extra $17,000 a year in pension for the rest of my life."

"I see," I said, pondering what this might mean to us and our developing timetable.

"But," he said, filling in my short pause for reflection . . .

"If you need me now, I'll come."

I nodded, "OK," still trying to keep my cards somewhat close to the vest. That's just how I've learned to operate, and I've found it serves me well. But I told him later, after he and his family had finally come and gotten settled here—and man, what a great bunch of people they are—"Nothing you ever said or did, Jonathan, in any of our time together, did more to show me what I was looking for than when you said, 'I'm willing to walk,' even if it means losing that much money by just a few months." He was more interested in making a long-term investment in his children, their experiences, and their future than could be measured by dollar signs alone.

(Although we did gladly honor his request.)

What are you willing to give up, even if it seems to make the most sense for your career, even if it folds nicely into your ambitions, even if it fulfills a dream you always wanted to come true for yourself, when perhaps it's not the best investment to make in your primary role as a husband or wife, as a father or mother—if its main multiplier will reside in *you* but not in them?

I understand how some of these matters can skirt along within gray areas of indecision, where the practical application of wisdom and prayer is undeniably needed. I realize in the rough-and-tumble of daily life, when you're tired and overwhelmed and not always thinking as clearly as you mean to be, you can make misjudgments in certain areas, sometimes in significant areas. All of us do. But your commitment to knowing and being *who you are* will work for you in helping these various calls pay off for you and your family in the long run.

If love can cover "a multitude of sins" (1 Pet. 4:8), a commitment to being a multiplier can overcome a whole bunch of stray losses and subtractions.

"For where your treasure is, there your heart will be also" (Matt. 6:21).

Higher Math

I was in one of our local Blockbuster video stores one evening, trying to find a movie to watch later that night. Speaking of Blockbuster—never in my life, I believe, have I witnessed an industry's entire life cycle from beginning to end, watching it sprout up from nothing, reach iconic proportions of success, and then just tumble off the face of the earth, all in a matter of—what, twenty-five years or so? I remember when there was no such thing as a Blockbuster store. And I remember when there was no such thing as a little town in America that didn't have one. And now, good luck if you can find a brick-and-mortar video rental store anywhere in the country. We saw Blockbuster go from birth to death, open to close—because that's not the way we consume our entertainment anymore. Welcome to the new speed of doing business.

But if you can travel back in your mind's eye to Friday nights when all the new, hot releases were stacked along the walls in plastic VHS or DVD shells, and whatever choice you made was due back by that same time or sooner on Sunday—for $4.99—then you can picture the scene where I was located when I heard this deep voice booming from over my right shoulder, saying, "Hey, Mr. John."

I looked around. It was Tommy.

"You remember me?" he asked.

Of course I remembered Tommy. So do you. He's the guy I told you about who had written those suggestive letters to the girl in school, whose mother had come over to the house that night and ripped him a new one, right there in our living room. "Thanks," he'd told me after she left, fuming at me in anger, "no one's ever stood up for me before." Remember that story?

Well, say hello again to Tommy, now six feet four inches and well over two hundred pounds, just a mountain of a man. It had been a long time.

"You got a minute?" he asked me.

"Sure."

He ducked off down one of the nearby aisles, called to someone, and in seconds was back with his arm around a young woman he wanted to introduce me to. "This is Mr. John," he said to her, after telling me her name.

"Nice to meet you," I said.

And as unforgettable as those words of Tommy's had become to me from so many years ago, the next words his wife spoke were equally as timeless. I don't know what all she could've said, just in making polite conversation. Could've told me where they lived, could've told me about other people we knew in common, could've told me what movie they'd picked out for the night. Anything. Instead, in the space of four simple words, she summed up the miracle that can happen when you and I choose to make our investments in other people instead of in our personal goals, awards, money, and stuff.

"I'd like you to meet my wife," Tommy had said to me. And the first thing she thought to say, while shaking my hand in both of hers, looking intently in my eyes, was . . . this:

"He's a *good* man."

Whew. That's my payday.

I didn't need a Blockbuster video anymore to get my weekend off to a great start. All I needed were those four simple words from a woman who was not only standing in front of me but was standing in the next decimal place over, in a multiplication equation that God had led us to help solve years ago in the life of a young boy who simply needed a chance.

And watch out. Because it was about to get even better.

"And this is my daughter," Tommy said, hoisting a little girl to eye level, who'd jumped into his arms when he bent down to pick her up.

"You're him?" she asked me, cute as a button.

"Yeah, I guess," I said.

Then here you go again. Listen to what she said. Such simple words. And every one of them feeling like they weighed as much as a ton of gold yet at the same time were lighter than air to my soul. "I love my daddy," she said, so sweetly and sincerely, before hopping down and running off.

Ching, ching.

Add that paycheck to the running total.

It's like pushing that multiplication button again.

"We've got to go," Tommy finally said. "Good to see you."

"You too, buddy. Thanks for letting me meet your family."

He reached out and shook my hand. Paused just a second more.

"I never forgot. Thank you."

No. Thank *you*.

Lord, thank *You*.

You and me, we've got problems we're trying to juggle every day. Work problems. Family problems. Money problems.

Time-management problems. Problems in some of our relationships, in some of our plans for the future. Problems are just a
part of life, part of every day. But if we can see them instead as
multiplication problems—opportunities to bring out the best in
others, to make decisions that bless and invest in our children,
our families, our churches, our neighbors, our customers, our
coworkers. When we do that, I've seen God take great interest
in being sure we're adequately supplied with both the wisdom
and resources to channel His love and goodness into everyone's
best welfare.

So sharpen the point on your pencil, and sharpen your focus
on other people. And before you know it, you'll be dealing with
higher math than any of us are capable of understanding, and
yet you'll be reaping and sharing the kind of results that none
of us can contain.

CHAPTER 9

Reach

You're Not by Yourself

Some things, the minute you hear them, just sound right. Even if you're not sure exactly how to get started, even if you've never given it a whole lot of thought before—and even if you know from past experience that you would probably have a hard time following through on it very well—you're nonetheless totally convinced. You know it's something you should be doing. You feel kind of foolish, in fact—maybe even a little guilty—for not having seen it more clearly until now. But with this rekindled motivation underneath you, with fresh fire in the belly, you truly want to change your attitudes and habits to better embrace it as your own new resolution, from now on.

And when we talk about something like wanting to multiply ourselves in others' lives, as we did in the last chapter, wanting to enlarge and inspire people to new heights of achievement, most of us feel the tug to do that. We get it. We're all for it. We want this to be who we are: people who make a difference in people.

So isn't it strange that a similar idea—one that's basically just the flip side of the same coin—might sound to some of us as if it means settling for something we sort of wish we could avoid. The notion of needing other people to help us, or else we're likely to come up short of our goals, can seem like a little bit of a downer, in one way of judging it. Our culture, in many regards, trains us to be independent minded and self-supporting. We'd rather figure things out by ourselves, if we can. It's the same mentality that keeps us from stopping to ask for directions or going next door again to get advice on a do-it-yourself project. Sort of defeats the whole do-it-yourself purpose, doesn't it?

We want to be the smart one.

Not the needy one.

But any objection we feel (if we do) toward expecting our success to involve others' assistance should cause us to question why we're so quick to bristle at it. Because if we see the noble quality that's inherent in multiplying ourselves through others, we should just as readily accept the equally noble partnership that occurs when others do their multiplying through us.

Make sense?

Of course it does. And that's why when people ask if I ever get tired of begging for money to help maintain the vision and stability of Big Oak Ranch, I tell them I've never begged for anything a day in my life. To beg would mean not trusting God's faithfulness to provide for our kids. To beg would mean I don't think telling their story is enough to motivate people to come alongside us. To beg would mean I believe the Ranch is more about me than about them. It's not.

But I fully expect to need help. I don't make any bones about it. I'm under no delusions as to why we've been able to keep bringing hope to these couple of thousand kids down through the years.

Lots of other people are why.

Lots and lots of people make this happen.

So I tell folks all the time, "Sure, I'm going to use you, but I'm going to use you for our kids." That's how I look at it. I'm as honored to serve these children as I'm honored by other people wanting to serve them through me, through us. And I believe that's an important place for you and me to set up shop in life. Both multiplying and being multiplied. A sizable share of the freedom, joy, fulfillment, and significance we all desire—though far too many of us ever experience it—is found in living right there in between those two complementary positions.

Both giving *and* receiving.

Trust me, I've seen what happens. In all my forty years of going out and talking about these boys and girls that we've taken in as our own, no one has ever—I mean not one single person—asked to be sure their gift would qualify them for a tax break. I'm not saying their IRS returns don't reflect their contribution and enable them to benefit from it, but that's not the nudge behind why people give to the Ranch. They hear about our children, or they meet one of them, and then, honestly, I don't need to ask anymore. They just get the picture, and they want to come on board. Or if they don't, that's fine with me because I know the Lord will send somebody else.

And I'm just as certain that if the dreams in your heart are as big as He usually designs them to be, you won't be capable of doing it all in your basement or without seeing it become way too complicated for you to pull off by your own smarts and instincts. But by choosing to be comfortable with *who you are*, by believing in Him as the one who has birthed these desires inside your heart, you'll soon get over the arrogance of thinking you're above needing help or embarrassed to welcome others' voices and investments in you. All you'll want is whatever brings the most glory to God and whatever involves the just-right people He's calling to be part of what He's doing in you, same as you've been invited to be part of doing it for others.

Because once we're there—once the pride-breathing, privacy-loving, pretend side of ourselves is finished trying to create our lives in our own image—then the extent of our reach can go far beyond the outstretched lunge of our fingertips, and maybe even beyond the stretches of our craziest imagination.

Why should we ever want to do *anything* that seeks to limit what God has started? That's stupid.

People ask Brodie a lot, now that he's transitioning into more and more leadership responsibilities around here, "How do you envision Big Oak Ranch changing in the years to come?" He'll usually shoot back with a quick answer—not testy but pretty tightly wound: "I think it would be mighty arrogant of me to come in here and say, 'Well, I see us going in a new direction.' I'm not saying it's perfect. I mean, if you're not getting better, you're getting worse. But do you think my dad, forty years ago, saw us having two separate ranches, nineteen homes, our own school that we run, and a steady stream of 140 kids that we'd be raising at any one time? No. He didn't see all that. I think he would have said, 'All I know is what God has laid on my heart. Why don't we just sit back and see where He decides to take it?'"

Darn straight.

And what the Ranch will look like forty years from now—under Brodie and Reagan's leadership, and then under somebody else's when the time is right—will most likely be as jaw-dropping as its present structure would've seemed to me at twenty-three.

Only one way this is going to happen, however—by fully anticipating and counting on the gracious, generous partnership of those who will always feel drawn to participate in things that exist in God's wheelhouse and are therefore changing people's lives.

So bring 'em on. Get out there among people you can learn from and grow with. Develop a desire for cooperating rather than lone-rangering. Seek out people who inspire you and whose interaction in your life consistently make you better, rather than gravitating backward toward those who veer you off-course, confuse the clarity of your goals, or lower your sense of determination. Keep your heart tested against those who can hold you accountable.

And together we'll outreach our wildest dreams.

Start of Something Special

I was the first sophomore in our high school ever to play on the varsity basketball team.

I remember my first game, which came against one of the big powerhouse schools in our region. We were trailing by only one point, down to our last possession. And me, being a lowly sophomore, was the only guy on the floor that the other team had intentionally left unguarded, thinking I was pretty harmless standing over there all by myself, especially behind the half-court line. But with nobody else open to throw to, the ball ended up in my hands, almost by default. With two seconds left I flung up a prayer from fifty feet out, and—wonder of wonders—it went in. At the buzzer. We won. My first game.

"Boy," I thought, "this high school basketball is pretty fun!"

As I told you before, Coach Bostick had us really cooking by my junior season, the time when (in the old days, at least) the college recruitment letters would start rolling in if athletic programs were interested in you. Three of us in my class at Gadsden High would ultimately sign to play on scholarship at major colleges—one in basketball, two in football. So just about every day in eleventh grade, the intercom would crackle at some point with the announcement, "We've got letters here for John Croyle. Please come to the office."

So I got the hint of a reputation for being a little arrogant. Big Man on Campus. I didn't think I was, but people are always quick to form their impressions, especially in the inferiority jungle known as high school. There was this one girl, though—Teresa Smith, a good friend of mind—who I noticed would come to my defense when people were talking about me. "If he's arrogant," she'd say, "he's got good reason to be. Leave him alone."

I always liked that girl.

Liked her enough to eventually marry her!

And when I think about how God has so faithfully brought partners into my life to keep the Ranch churning and rolling and coming together into what He wanted it to be, my wife, Tee, is and will always be the one I could never do without.

Because, see, I was *called* to do this. To build a children's home. But Tee—she *chose* it. She could've easily kept on dating the guy she was seeing in college who looked like a poster model, who was kind and good and everything a girl could want. But she changed gears and opted instead for the tall, ugly guy with the five boys tagging around after him.

Kids have asked me if Tee and I ever messed around before we got married. Wasn't much chance of that. How *could* we? We had five teenagers out with us on every date.

But that's what she chose.

And God knew exactly what He was doing when she did.

"A man who finds a wife," the Bible says, "finds a good thing and obtains favor from the LORD" (Prov. 18:22). Amen to that. And I would say to you: before you put too much stock in what others tell you, before you go out hoping to get people to buy into who you are and what you can do, be sure you've got this one relationship right. She needs to be what makes you click. She needs to be the one who causes you to want to reach the straightest and farthest.

Not everyone marries, I know. And not everyone who's been married is still married today. I understand that. But if you're blessed enough to have a wife—or if you're a woman, blessed enough to have a husband—treat this special person with your one-of-a-kind brand of love and loyalty. Because if any partner ever becomes more important to you than *that* partner, you're headed for the worst trouble in your life. You'll be hamstrung from reaching the places you're designed to reach if you lean more heavily on someone else's advice, ideas, and influence than that of your spouse. I've made that mistake once or twice along the way, and heaven help me from ever making it again.

No one knows me like Tee does. No one possesses the full information to be able to say to me what she can. And when others bring out the long knives in criticizing me, no one is quicker to jump to my defense than she is.

Choose your mate well.

And choose your mate always.

Proceeding in Partnership

With your family centering you, with your roots driven deep, you can be your most real and your most genuine. You can slough off this uppity persona that wants to prove how fully intelligent and independent you are. And then, in honesty and in better touch with reality, you're ready for God to branch you out into all kinds of exciting, equipping directions.

Because, hear me now—I may be a big talker who can cut up and get other people sold on what I'm excited about. But there is no special reason God has brought so many hands, shoulders, backs, and elbows to the task of Big Oak Ranch, other than the fact that He is good to His children. And since I know—I *know!*—that you have been created with specific intention for the purpose of drawing maximum glory to God, I know your prayers for help will not go unheeded. Your patience, your faith, and your openness in trusting His wise awareness of exactly what you need will result in your receiving it.

So in sharing the following few examples of how He's mobilized others around us, I'm not meaning to amaze for the sake of good storytelling. To the contrary, I think I'm just reporting on what God considers to be normative. The way His kingdom works, according to what His Word promises, He assembles our full supply of resources as a matter of course when we cooperate with Him in faith. He reaches in and kindles the fire in us and in others for doing His will.

Brodie, for example, was out on a hunting trip with several other businessmen. And at one point in their outing, being the kind of guys who deal every day in big numbers, the subject came up—wonder how much it costs to operate a place like ours? Answer: *a lot.*

One of the men on this outing was a person Brodie had known for many years, a longtime friend whose company is in the gasoline business. And later on, as they sat down for a meal, he said to Brodie, "I've been thinking, and I believe I can help you with your gasoline expenses." Before long, he'd sent out the equipment to install two big fuel tanks, supplying both of our ranches, and set up standard gas-station pumps that our houseparents and our maintenance crews—anyone who puts miles on their car or needs gas for their mower on Ranch business—can access with a personalized card swipe. Tells who's getting what, when, and where, for accountability purposes. Then when the fuel in the tank has dipped below a certain level, a computer chip embedded inside alerts the home office, who sends out a truck to top it off again. Free gas. Can't beat it.

Saves us many, many, many thousands of dollars every month.

It's another clear example of God's faithfulness to us.

Another incredible partner to praise Him for.

And another real blessing for our kids.

One of many.

Like, for example, the partner who now supplies all our breakfast meats and pork products for the kids and families at the Ranch. Never asked him. He just did it.

We'd been working hard to make ourselves completely self-sufficient on our farm-grown meat and poultry. The kids, as part of their chores and work assignments, had been investing their time in raising cattle, raising chickens (to the tune of a hundred eggs or more a day), and also raising hogs. But the guy on our staff who was in charge of the hog program put a pencil to what we were investing in feed and care, versus the yield we were producing, and suggested it might be costing us more to raise our own pork than to buy it in bulk.

Plus it would certainly smell better.

And so we had just, within the past two weeks, made the decision to pull the plug on it—when a local business owner came to us and said he'd like to supply us with whatever we need as far as bacon, sausage, ham, pork chops, baloney, all kinds of frozen and refrigerated pork. He said, "As long as we own the company"—which will basically be forever since it's been a family-run business for generations—"we'll provide you with as much as you need."

First Tuesday of every month, a truck pulls up to the Ranch with twenty-two hundred pounds of breakfast meat, and we help load it into our industrial-size, walk-in coolers and freezers that keep all our families stocked with food.

Another blessing for our kids.

And there are just so many more to tell.

Laguna Beach Christian Retreat in Panama City, Florida, has allowed us to bring down the whole Ranch—kids, staff, and all our families—for nearly as long as we've been in existence. Even when the companies that own the place have changed hands, a permanent clause in the contract states that at the end of the season, every summer, the children of Big Oak Ranch can come and stay for a week. For free.

The folks who run it now—children of the previous own-
ers—not only host all 220 of us for our week's vacation, but on
one of the nights while we're there, they cook a huge meal for
us, feed us like family. And love every minute of it. They also
broker with a nearby beach-toy business to give us a huge break
on rentals of, you know, skimboards and inflatables and things
with wild, colorful sails on them. Big fun on the water. The
owner of that business, by the way, loves our kids so much, that
he and his wife and their two children came up to see us recently
after we'd just been down there and said, "I've never seen anything like this." Turned around and wrote us a check for $5,000.

Like I said, our kids speak for themselves.

A family who runs a thirty-six-hundred-acre hunting pre-
serve, not too far from us, lets our children come over and hunt
there. No telling how many of our boys have gotten their first
deer during one of those early Saturday mornings. I'd say we
harvest thirty or forty nice-sized does and bucks every time we
go. We're never charged a thing.

One of the finest psychiatrists in the area donates his time to
provide counseling expertise with our kids who need what his
skills can offer. Reagan had been so impressed with him and his
practice, she had talked with our business director about agree-
ing to a monthly retainer we could pay him for his services and
had approached him to see if he'd be interested. Would be *willing*, is a better word for it, because it still wasn't much money.
"Funny you should mention it," he said to her, "because I've
been praying about it and . . . yes, I want to do it. And no, you're
not paying me."

We've also been blessed with a number of what we call
resource families and relief families who serve a major ministry
component in the kids' lives. *Resource families* step into the role
of being sort of like an aunt and uncle to our children, a home
they can go visit on every-so-often weekends just to get away
and be treated like welcomed, loving company. *Relief families*,

you might say, minister more directly to our houseparents, coming into one of our homes and taking care of *all* the kids so the parents can get away by themselves for a few days.

A local grocery distributor donates several thousands of dollars worth of food every week—products that may have been dented or scuffed up a little, perhaps overstocked and needing to be discarded. But over here we've certainly got enough mouths to feed and clothes to wash—we don't need too much wiggle room ahead of the sell-by date to thoroughly empty out the contents. And we sure don't mind popping out the plastic on a gouged bottle of dishwashing liquid or ignoring the weathered look of a few soup cans that had a hard ride on the shipping pallet coming over.

What a blessing for our kids, all these things.

What would we do without partners like these?

But what I really want you to see in reading our stories are not the dollar amounts and the right-on-time deliveries of provision that God has never failed to give to us. Yes, these friends of the Ranch—and so many others—help our few little arms reach all the way around this place and around our children, and still stay roomy enough to keep bringing new kids into our home and family who don't have anybody else to care about them. Yet just by doing what God has called us to do—by being who we are—He actually makes these people's partnership in our work exactly what *they* need too.

The president of a cabinetmaking company, a number of years ago, was sitting in a tense, come-to-Jesus meeting with his accountant. Revenue had been slowing to a trickle, and unexpected cost overruns were fighting whatever gains they'd hoped to achieve in their best-case scenario projections. Time was running out, and the money just wasn't there. They couldn't make payroll, and hard decisions were needing to be made.

Laying down his reading glasses on the stack of papers, leaning back in his chair, and succumbing to a visible slouch in his shoulders, the man turned to his money guy and said, behind closed, tired eyes, "I know what's wrong."

"What's that?"

Pausing a moment to let the thought completely settle, he opened his eyes and steadfastly answered, "We haven't been tithing."

Hmm?

"That's right. We've been so worried about surviving, we've quit being serious about giving."

Today that company has more than a million square feet of industrial and office space under roof, employing as many as a thousand people in their manufacturing operation. And one of the reasons God has restored them to prominence and profitability is through His blessing on their support of Big Oak Ranch. Even when times were tough during some of the economic struggles of the past decade, when slowdowns in new construction forced them to trim staff by several hundred people in order to keep going, they've continued to be steady supporters of ours.

Helping *us* to reach farther has helped *them* to reach as well.

Same thing goes, I believe, for the old boy who runs one of the local bars here in town. He was familiar with the work we do at the Ranch from our exposure in the community, from TV and all, from just driving by and—I don't know, getting a vibe in his heart, not knowing it was probably the Holy Spirit.

He called me one day, told me who he was, and asked if I'd be willing to meet him in the Kmart parking lot at a certain hour the next day.

"Sure," I said. "Happy to."

He told me what kind of car he'd be driving. I pulled up, got out, made our acquaintance, said hello.

"The reason I wanted to meet you here," he said, "was because I didn't want people to see you with me."

"Really?"

"Well, you know—what I do for a living."

"Oh, yeah, sure, I . . . understand."

"But I've heard a lot about you, Mr. Croyle, and what y'all do. I think it's really great. And, uh," taking an envelope out of his pocket, he said, "I've got some money here that I'd like to give you . . . if, well . . . I don't know. Do you take money from people like me?"

"Mister," I said, popping my right hand into his, "Jesus gave money to somebody out of the mouth of a fish. And I'd say you're worth a whole lot more than a fish."

Can we and our kids use that man's money? Absolutely.

But I think giving it to *us* did something special for *him* as well.

What I'm saying is: when you keep yourself content and in line with who God has made you to be, when you truly want His will to take place "on earth as it is in heaven"—including on the little plot of earth that's right there under your own two feet—He'll make sure you're never lacking for whatever gives you the necessary reach to serve Him. And because He's not confined to one-dimensional, one-directional ways of thinking, this also means that others' investments and cooperation with you are not simple additions to one person and takeaways from another. Just as we're free to stand squarely between giving and receiving, God builds into each act of giving the accompanying properties of receiving blessing, and He builds into each received gift the ability to give back.

Everyone profits. Everyone benefits.

Everyone reaches for the win.

Let It Stretch You

Like with a lot of nonprofits, we've been blessed with a number of faithful donors who believe in what we're doing and who put their time and money where their heart is. Because of their amazing generosity and commitment, our kids are able to take advantage of some incredible opportunities to stretch, grow, excel, and achieve.

You know who you are.

And I thank God for you.

But when I'm sitting here making decisions about how to spend my day, when I'm faced with challenges and travel and a schedule that sometimes calls me beyond what my body and attention span feel ready to tackle, I usually think of one special donor in particular who makes me want to dig down and reach for every ounce of kid-focused energy I can muster.

Month in and month out, without fail, this little old lady sends us her gift.

Two dollars.

Every time.

She even wrote me a note once, a little yellow sticky attached to her creased dollar bills. It said, "Thank you for letting me help your kids. I really appreciate the BRE (business reply envelope). That forty-five cents really helps." No postage necessary.

To which I say, *No problem, ma'am.*

I'm not meaning, now, to go all melodramatic over this woman's gift, like I don't realize it's only two dollars. Of course I do. (But remember the story of the widow's mite in the Bible.) I know two dollars doesn't stretch far enough to cover much more than a jug of iced tea. Barely pays the tax on a single package of socks and underwear. But if you don't think her gift does something extra special in the depths of my soul, if you don't think she has often come to mind at times when I was making a buying decision or was thinking about knocking off early and going home for the afternoon, then you don't know me very well. There's truly a lot more reach in those two dollars than their small size would suggest. No, they may not be enough to pay for even a new leaf rake, but I promise you, her money has touched just about every piece of ground on this property, through the excellence and devotion and spirit it helps to motivate in us.

That's no lie. No exaggeration.

It really doesn't take much to make a difference in others. And every time somebody chooses to build a little something extra into you, receive it with gratitude for what it is, no matter how seemingly small and inconsequential. It's a gift from God, and it's meant to cause a reaction in you.

It's meant to help you reach out for the next rung.

CHAPTER 10

Care

You're Here to Serve

"Even the Son of Man did not come to be served, but to serve, and to give His life—a ransom for many" (Mark 10:45).

I realize the whole Bible is inspired by God and is worthy of our reading, intended for our instruction—even, I guess, those long family history parts in places like Numbers and Chronicles, where we learn about men whose fathers apparently thought nothing of giving them Dr. Seuss-sounding names like Ziph and Ziza and Ziklag.

Some verses, however, are the kind that say everything in just a few brief words. And Mark 10:45 is certainly one of those. The fact that Jesus Himself, when He came to Earth, arrived with the dedicated purpose of *serving* . . . I think we can all agree, based on this, that none of us is getting far with the argument that cleaning the bathroom is not our job.

Serving is everybody's business.

Being a servant needs to be *who you are*.

Nobody needs to be too big for their own britches. Nobody gets to be somebody important by lording their position or their status over other people and trying to control them. "Whoever would be great among you," Jesus said, "must be your servant" (Matt. 20:26 ESV).

That's why one of the greatest compliments anyone ever paid to me came from a guy who was visiting Brodie here at the Ranch—a man who, even though he was a big-time executive, understood this truth we're talking about . . . and knew it when he saw it. "I've been in CEOs' offices all over the world," he said to my son, "and they always have stuff on their walls about what *they've* done, what *they've* accomplished. What I liked when I went into your office, and into your dad's office, was that I didn't see one thing that talked about what *you'd* won or what *you'd* been honored with. All I saw were pictures of your family and pictures of the Big Oak kids."

Of course.

What else am I here to do?

I've been the boss around this place for forty years. So what? What's that supposed to mean? That I get the best parking spot? That nobody can make me do anything I don't want to do? That everybody bows and scrapes and gives me all the credit for starting this thing up and making it what it is today?

No.

I'm here, just like everybody else is here—to serve.

To serve our kids.

And as you look at your own life, I ask you to run your attitude up the same kind of flagpole. Or should I say, *totem pole.* You've seen the images of a Native American totem pole—the carved faces, the eagle's wings, the various depictions of tribal lore. Most people, thinking in typical pecking-order fashion, would figure that the representations that appear on top would be the ones of greatest importance. But from what I've heard and read, the opposite is often the case. The portion that portrays the highest-ranking person (or god or spirit or whatever) is actually the one at the bottom. The "low man on the totem pole" is ironically the one ascribed the greater honor.

So no matter how much money you make, who your parents are, what your job title says, where your degree is from, what kind of car you drive, how nice your clothes look on you, what your online profiles say about you, how many marathons you've run—it just really couldn't matter any less. Your business going out the door today is to serve God and to serve the people you'll be coming into contact with. *Period.*

Now the unpleasant part of this mandate is that it might get your hands dirty. It might force you to work through your lunch hour. It might take you to a couple of different shopping places in afternoon traffic trying to find the right item that somebody asked you to pick up. It might cause you to do some things that feel at first as if they're beneath your dignity.

But the good part is, it ought to really simplify things for you.

You're the servant; *they're* the ones to be served.

And the Bible calls that kind of attitude . . .

Grr-reat.

Without a Care

I think I know why this subject of caring and serving hits me at such a gut level. And it's not because I'm so incredible at doing it. Like you I get tired. I get to thinking I've earned some time to myself. I don't always feel like caring whether somebody else has got what they need—have they not noticed that I don't have what *I need*?

(Probably just me who thinks that. Not you.)

But when I think about what it means to care for another person, I start flipping through a camera roll in my head of nearly two thousand kids I've grown to know and love throughout the balance of my adult life. And while I'm eternally grateful that God has given us what we need at Big Oak Ranch to be a source of encouragement and blessing to them, I hate that because of a past that they had little to no control over, they've ever had to experience the rejection of not being cared about.

I think of one of our boys who texted a picture to his dad of a deer he'd shot recently. A little four-point buck. No real trophy for the wall or anything. But still—anytime you get one, it's a big deal. And even if your buddies might give you a good ribbing for bagging such a ferocious beast, you at least figure your father will be impressed.

He wasn't. Instead, his dad sent him a return text not too much later, which said, "That's nothing. Here, let me show you mine."

Didn't care.

Didn't get it.

I think of one of our girls whose sister, years before, had tried to choke her one day at home. And her parents, instead of being upset with the sister for attacking her, started beating up on *her* instead. Beat her unconscious, in fact. They were mad at *her* because she'd made her *sister* mad. How backwards is that?

When her father died a few years later, she went to the funeral, of course, and told her mom the only thing of her dad's that she really wanted was his Bible. So they went and found it and gave it to her. But then the little sister decided she wanted it more, and the mom came and took it away from the older girl. Tore out what little was left of her daughter's heart. Unbelievable.

I remember that same girl telling me, after she'd graduated from high school, how one of her classmates a year or two earlier—some stupid boy—had gotten in a mouthy argument with her about something. And for his low-blow parting shot at a defenseless girl, he chose this dandy little punch: "Well, at least I've *got* parents."

"Angry" really isn't a good enough word to describe my feelings when she shared this story. He and *his* parents had better be glad I wasn't aware of that altercation until long after he was out from under my say-so at the school because I would've ended it for him a whole lot sooner. I'm not the hammer very often, but I promise you, if I had known about it in time, his tenure as a Westbrook student would've been the nail. And I would've countersunk it in one blow. Imagine, having come from the background this girl grew up in, having a fruitcake for a mother and now a father who's dead, and having to listen to some snide, gutless remark from a snotty-headed boy who even on his *worst* day had never had a *bad* day.

I don't like what I've seen from people who don't care.

People who don't care about our kids.

Having operated a place like ours for as long as we've done it, we've pinpointed the most common times of year when parents decide to bail on their children. We count on it like the turn of the seasons. *Dump zones,* we call them. And the timing of these trends does a good job of revealing exactly what and who these parents really care about.

The first one—the worst one—is Christmas, as I've mentioned a couple of times already. I can't really figure that one out. Like you I just can't get my mind to go there—to whatever could make a parent want to kick their kid out of the house the week before Christmas. It's usually not a money problem, I can tell you—as if they can't afford what Christmas entails. Even if they can't, that's not the real reason. It's just . . . they're done. They've had it. They don't care.

The second one is the end of school. This past year five new kids showed up within two days after classes let out in the spring, eleven in two weeks. I guess it's just because summer's coming. There's nobody to watch the kids all day long anymore. So get rid of 'em. Let somebody who cares take care of them.

The third one is the *start* of school. They don't want to have to fool with homework. Don't want to have to buy books and clothes. Don't want to have to drive them back and forth places, here and there.

Then sometimes, of course, we'll get a call from a parent who says they made a mistake. They dropped little Billy off here last month, but they've been seriously reconsidering, they say, and they'd like to come back and take him home. Didn't realize what they were doing.

"Oh, the check stopped, huh? Social Security check? Didn't see that coming, did you?"

They just don't care. About anybody but themselves.

It kills you.

That's why we end up with a lot of little girls like Zoe, for example—six years old, sweet little thing. Her new housemom, soon after Zoe arrived, had walked her over to the little boutique at the Ranch where we keep clothes sized, marked, and ready to go. But something in this housemother's heart just wasn't finding what she wanted for her new little daughter. Some of it was fine, but it wasn't enough. Not for this one.

So she took her out to a . . . not a high-end store or anything, but a mid-level place. Found her a pretty pink dress that made her little freckled face gleam like a lighthouse. "I tell you, Mr. John, there wasn't any way in the world I wasn't going to buy that dress for her. The look on her face—if it had cost $1,000, I would've found some way to give it to her."

That night—her first night—they had eaten together as a family, cleaned away the supper dishes, gone about the evening's routine, and then watched as the hour crept closer to bedtime. Zoe's new mom came in, scooped her up, carried her upstairs, and put her into bed. Zoe peeked back at her from beneath the bedcovers, smiled her infectious little grin, and said, "Thank you."

"Thank you for what?"

"My whole life I've dreamed that someone would tuck me in at night."

She was still wearing that dress.

And you're telling me some parent couldn't see anything in that little girl to care about? Are you kidding me? Nothing worth sacrificing for? Nothing worth wanting to delight with a mother's love? Nothing worth even going into her room and kissing her goodnight?

We think life is so complicated. And I know sometimes it really is. But bottom line, our main reason for breathing oxygen into these two lungs of ours is to serve, to love, and to care.

I'm sick of seeing what happens when people don't.

The Many Faces of Caring

Nothing much does my father's heart any prouder than when my daughter Reagan comes to tell me about a new boy or girl she's brought in. I can hear from just the tone in her voice how passionately she feels about rescuing another child from almost certain destruction.

And then my son Brodie—he might not want me to put this in print because it's not exactly torn from the NFL playbook. But one of the proudest moments of my life involved something I saw him do, even though it occurred in the midst of a truly sad, distressing moment.

One of our girls, after repeated efforts to help her, had continued to prove unable to adjust to our structure and rules. I won't go into all the details, but, suffice to say, we had no other choice than to find her a different kind of living environment. The decision, despite its difficulty, was not a hard one to make. She'd basically made it *for* us.

And she knew it. "I know I'm messed up, Mr. Brodie," she said, the inner warfare seeping out through her weary, tormented tears. "But I'm going to get some help. I'm going to get better. And one day—I mean it—I'm going to come back."

And my son, once she was gone—my man's man son—fell completely to pieces. I'd hardly ever seen him shed a single tear before. But on that day, having lived out that kind of intense, dramatic scene, he sobbed for the first time in his life.

"Dad," he said, "I'd told her when she first came that we wouldn't quit on her."

"I know, son. I understand. But we can't give her what she needs right now."

And yet what I saw wrestling inside him was the kind of love, dedication, and caring that every man I know would want to see in his child.

It does my heart good to know both of our children possess this type of love in the depths of their very soul.

So just as being around our Ranch kids has given me painful, front-row access to the many awful varieties human cruelty and callousness can take, it's also frequently put me in the same room with some of the most muscular acts of caring I can imagine.

A lot of it branches into our life from people who serve as true multipliers of our ministry—like the resource families I briefly talked about in the last chapter. Try to place yourself, for example, in the position of a nineteen-year-old boy coming home from college for the weekend. If he was yours, he'd show up on Friday afternoon with a few of his things tossed into an overnight bag or backpack. Then after a taste of mama's cooking at supper and probably a night out with a couple of his old high school friends, he'd slip back in at 11:00 or 11:30, tiptoe into his room, and stretch out in his own bed till way past sunrise the next morning.

But what about *our* nineteen-year-olds who come home from college for a long weekend? The room where they grew up is now occupied by a seven-year-old who came here three months ago, who's receiving the same opportunity this college kid enjoyed throughout most of his childhood. So does that mean the nineteen-year-old is better off just staying at school and never coming home?

No—because he's had a nearby family who made a place for him three or four times a year his whole life. During those weekends at their house, they cooked him pancakes and sausage on Saturday mornings. Took him to the zoo, the park, let him stay up late with their other kids and clown around, making up stuff to do and playing video game tournaments. Took him to church on Sunday, and then fed him another big meal before bringing him back to the Ranch later on that afternoon. Tons of fun. Loads of good memories. They've been like family to him.

And a lot of times, when our kids want a real bed to sleep in on a college-getaway weekend, they might just call up the loving, caring family who's been offering them getaway weekends all their lives.

What a tremendous example of serving and caring.

Then sometimes the caring comes back from the nineteen-year-old kids themselves. I ran into one of our guys who'd left us after high school and was out on his own. We talked and caught up for a few minutes. And as we shook hands and prepared to say good-bye, I said to him, "By the way, Scott—thank you. For last Christmas."

"Aww," he said.

"No, I mean it. What you did is important." He had sent us a few hundred dollars to sponsor a couple of our kids for the holidays.

"Well . . . those kids were *me*, five years ago. Somebody did it for me."

"Yeah, but I just want to tell you, I'm really proud of you for that."

He looked down again, sort of embarrassed by the compliment. "I've made a lot of mistakes," he said, "but I really appreciate what y'all did for me."

Appreciated it enough not to just take it and run with it, but to stop . . . and to care.

Our kids do that all the time.

So we try to keep our eyes peeled for opportunities, not just to do what our children need but to go that little bit extra to make sure they really know we care. Like the time one of our boys—one who'd had a really tough childhood—was sitting across the desk from me with his fiancé. He'd stopped by to introduce her to me, and we were just chatting, reminiscing.

People ask me sometimes, "So do y'all pay for your kids' weddings?" Yes. Don't you? I mean, traditionally, the bride's family pays for the bulk of the wedding expenses and details, right? And isn't that what we are, when one of our girls gets married? Her family? So the last three years, I think we've helped eight of our daughters plan and pay for their weddings.

Of course, we do.

But Paul and Becky here—this was a little different. He was one of our sons. So I just said, making conversation, "When are y'all getting married?"

"Oh, we're just," she said, reaching for his hand—"we're just going over to the justice of the peace."

She could tell I found this less than satisfactory.

"We'll be fine," she laughed. "It's OK."

"No, it's not," I said.

"Connie!" calling for my longtime assistant. She came gliding around the corner, into my office. "We need to get this girl a wedding dress."

"No! No!" Becky said, protesting.

Shushing her objections, I ran through what I was thinking with Connie, who soon returned to her desk to start making some phone calls. Then I rocked forward on my elbows, leaned across the desk, looked Becky and Paul straight in the eye, and said, "Go get married. We'll take care of your dress, your invitations, the food, it's covered. Let's do this right."

Not because we had to. Not because we'd planned it. Just because we care.

It's what we're here for. That's what you would do for your son.

Who Do You Think They Are?

Everybody's got a story, a background, a reason they do what they do. It may not be obvious to you. It may not even be obvious to *them* in some respects. They may not really have stopped to think about it. But anyone you meet today, I'll guarantee you—there's more to who they are than meets the eye.

Whoever they are, it's not just the person you see.

But we are so quick to size people up into small boxes. Make value judgments. Determine if this is someone who can help us, who can be used for our advantage, or if it's someone we can do without, who's not worth wasting our time on. We evaluate them based on our initial rattle of snapshots, looking at what people do, how they're dressed. We take stock of their appearance, guess their age, mark the sound of their speech and intelligence level, run them through the usual grid.

And we're wrong when we do that.

We're seeing them the way *we* want to see them.

And according to the Bible, not even *Jesus* does that.

"God did not send the Son into the world to judge the world," the Bible says, "but that the world might be saved through Him" (John 3:17 NASB). When the Son of God—the One who made heaven and earth—when He looks at someone, when He looks at us, He chooses to see us not as someone to compare Himself to but as someone He can serve and care for.

Could He do it differently? Uh, yes. Could He treat us like bugs to smash under His feet? Does He even need to notice us at all, as infinitesimal as we are, when compared with His eternal weight and range of glory?

Obviously He, now—unlike us—though stooping to serve us, is truly entitled to expect and demand our praise and worship. He is worthy of it. He made us. He made everything. He is God, the Ruler of all. But as for us, we don't deserve *anybody's* praise or deference, and we should know it. Not only are we shot through with stuff that's only useful for repentance, but anything we do, anything we've done, is only due to the skills, ability, temperaments, and opportunities Almighty God has given to us. As the Bible says, "What do you have that you didn't receive?" (1 Cor. 4:7)

So why should anybody, first impression, not strike us as a person to affirm, help, encourage, and respect? If presented with enough time and opportunity, why should we not take active steps to serve and assist them? Why should we always care so much more about our own plans, agendas, objectives, and timetables, and not give some serious consideration to what this other person might be lacking or suffering or praying for somebody's help with?

"For even the Son of Man did not come to be served, but to serve, and to give His life—a ransom for many" (Mark 10:45).

And I think that probably says it all, right there.

CHAPTER 11

Hope

You're Never Too Late

 Everybody has a story, like I said.

You, I know—you've got one too.

And after traveling through these forty years of life lessons with me, trying to match up the ones that seem to apply most directly to your own life, you might be feeling a need to do some work on that story of yours. I know I'm still working on mine.

So maybe, as you think about it, you've already been considering some light touch-ups and changes you'd like to start making to your average day. Little nips and tucks and good mental-note reminders. Healthy fine-tuning adjustments that, once you've tweaked them into place, ought to make your story read a little better, more like the way you've been wanting it to.

But what concerns me the most, as I interact with people from all different walks of life, is how many of them have decided that their story is not one that's really worth telling anymore. They've reached a point where their wastebasket is so full now of paper wads and trashed attempts at trying to write a satisfying story line for themselves, they've just tossed everything else in the garbage with it as well—the laptop, the power cord, the stapler, the coffeepot, the notes they've been working from, the pens and pencils . . . everything.

Forget it. It's over.

It's just too late now.

And if that's you, I ask you to hang in here with me for these few pages more because, I promise you, life is not over for you. You're not done.

I'm not denying that things have probably happened to you that may always exert their own brand of doubt and pressure on you, timed to catch you at your most exposed and vulnerable moments. Nor am I meaning to leave the impression that you (or anybody, for that matter) will ever be able to turn over enough new leaves until life suddenly reads like a page-turning adventure novel, with you as the daring, invincible hero. There will always be more "real" to our "real life" than any of us would prefer.

But I don't care if you're *twenty*-two and discouraged, sure that you've already blown it beyond all repair, or if you're *seventy*-two and discouraged, feeling no drive or energy anymore to clean up the mess that's been made, especially for what little good you think it'll do. Because either way, I'm telling you, it's never too late. As the old Chinese proverb says, "The best time for planting a tree was twenty years ago. The second best time is now."

The worst time is never.

Nobody needs the word *quitter* as part of their story.

The reason I give this little kick in the pants with such confidence is because I believe the entire message of the Bible and our personal application of it can be encapsulated into just two simple words: "*You can.*"

You can come home.

You can get back on track.

You can overcome your past.

You can act like the son or daughter of a King.

And so when I put my arm around one of these Big Oak kids in a group of other people, and I say, "Tell them who you are," what I'm really saying to that child, in essence, is, "You can."

You can be greater than some people's valuation of you.

You can overcome what you've done and endured.

You can stand up on your own two legs again.

You can be what you think you can't.

With God's help you can do it.

True, "You can do nothing *without* Me," Jesus said (John 15:5). No use in bucking the wisdom of that. But *with* Him, "all things are possible" (Matt. 19:26).

And, sorry, but I've read these verses and others that are just like them many times, and for the life of me, I don't see any limits imposed on them. Do you? No time limits, no jurisdiction limits, no frequency limits, no mileage limits. All I see are active, intact possibilities.

All I see is *hope.*

My college degree, in addition to reflecting my original major, which was English—(quit laughing)—also incorporates a secondary emphasis that I added later, a double major in religious studies. God in His wisdom, when He was directing me toward wanting to devote my life to helping at-risk children, gave me the insight as a junior in college to want to learn about what people believe and why they believe it. I figured if I could study the twelve or thirteen major religions of the world, including, of course, the largest ones—Christianity, Judaism, Islam, Hinduism, Buddhism—I could sit down with any kid in the world and know at least something about where he or she was coming from. And my experience through the years has proven again and again the benefit of having this knowledge on hand and at the ready.

But while a lot of people want to funnel each of these various streams of religious thought into one big God-ocean, concluding they're all just different colors and expressions of the same thing, the clear distinctives of Christianity result in one overarching takeaway that no other faith tradition can rightfully claim. Sure, they each possess certain beliefs; they each expect attentive devotion; they each deal in some way with man's sin and need and deficiencies. But when these other religions play all the way out, each one gags at a pivotal point.

I mean, watch enough people trying to bathe away the uncleanness of their soul in the Ganges River, or offer up to heaven an endless string of ritualistic prayers and fasting exercises, or navel-gaze their way to an ever elusive nirvana, and you can't help but recognize that even their best stabs at pleasing their deity (or their panorama of deities) always stops somewhere short of being possible.

Always comes up short of any realistic *hope*.

If hope is eternal, why can't it even make it until the weekend?

I got a letter recently from a teenage girl who's come to live with us in the past few months. I won't go into all of her backstory with you. I think you've gathered, from reading the book so far, the kinds of troubled, abusive years that have usually gone under the bridge by the time our kids come to the Ranch. Hers, I can tell you, was as bad and upsetting as anybody's. The stuff in her life hadn't only gone *under* the bridge but had flash-flooded over it and through it and pounded against it until there wasn't a whole lot of bridge left—which, considering where that bridge had led from, wasn't exactly a bad idea.

But if one sentiment came through to me as I was reading what she'd written, it was hope. The new hope she'd received from her houseparents and family. New hope telling her that old memories and thinking patterns were no longer in oppressive control over her. New hope in what she'd found and been given by God, who was proving Himself more loving and faithful than she'd ever known.

She was learning to trust people, she said. Was learning how to enjoy life rather than dreading it. She was changing and growing and expressing herself a little more easily and confidently each day and was experiencing a sense of freedom she'd pretty much given up on as being a viable possibility in her life anymore.

"I can finally be the real me," she said, "the loving, caring, and trustworthy me."

The real me.

Boy, those words stuck in my head for several days after reading them. *I can finally be the real me.* I know her years on the earth, relatively speaking, have been few until now, but, trust me, she's already lived a full lifetime in her small handful of experiences. And yet by stepping out into a position of hope, she can look back today at who she'd been before—how she felt, what she expected, how she responded to her various sets of stimuli—and tell it's not who she wanted to be.

It wasn't the real her.

And that's what I'm praying for you, if you feel like the hour's grown too late and you're too far gone to fix what's gone wrong, to repair or get past whatever's knocked you loose from being who you really are—who God really made you to be. Too late for that now? Why?

Too late to regain your sense of priority and focus?

Too late to start again with a long-haul mentality?

Too late to recapture a zeal for hardworking excellence?

Too late to pick the right battles and fight like a warrior?

Too late to live with expectation, trust, and faith?

Too late to commit to new habits and choices?

Too late to make a lasting difference in others?

Too late to believe you can reach your goals?

Too late to care, if you've quit really caring?

No, it's not too late. And hope is the reason. Hope is what readjusts your vision and perspective, despite whatever evidence appears to the contrary, and helps you see the real you again—even if the real you is somebody you've only heard about and wished for.

It's somebody you'd really like to meet.

And it's somebody you are still capable of being.

Hope Is Who You Are

Brodie, as a kid, when he and I would toss football in the late afternoons, testing his arm and his accuracy, envisioned himself going on to play at a highly competitive level. Like a lot of kids his age, whether they're dreaming of becoming an astronaut, a firefighter, a movie star, or a veterinarian, he faced the future with high expectations.

I remember him talking to me one time about how much better his chances of being seen and excelling would be if he could go play ball at the big 5A school down the road, not at our little Christian school that could barely (at the time) put enough boys on the field to constitute a team. You'd look down from the stands on a Friday night, and there'd be more of our players in the game than on the sidelines. But what if he was playing for a school that drew thousands of people every week and got big write-ups in the paper? What if he was handing off and throwing passes to guys like Carnel "Cadillac" Williams, his buddy who went on to star as running back for Auburn? Wouldn't that help show the scouts and recruiters what he was truly capable of doing?

"No," I told him. "If you're good enough, they'll find you," And sure enough, they did.

By the time he chose Alabama from among a long list of other suitors, those visions of starting at quarterback for the Crimson Tide continued to grow until they quickly became reality. But those years were a rocky patch for the usually stable and established football program at the University of Alabama. He ended up playing under four different coaches in his five years there, including his redshirt season as a freshman. He was recruited by Mike Dubose, played for Dennis Franchione (who left in the middle of the night for Texas A&M), practiced for Mike Price (who became embroiled in an off-the-field scandal and was fired before the season even started), and then finished up under Mike Shula.

In addition to the coaching carousel, Brodie also played hurt throughout most of his college career and into the pros. A separated shoulder here, a few cracked ribs and vertebrae there, a torn ACL and MCL and other body parts that need to be in some stage of working order for quarterbacks to do their job—which, among other things, requires standing on a golf tee while a 330-pound lineman with a running start picks you up and plants you in the ground. Oh, and standing there and throwing a precision ball while he's doing it.

Boy, did he ever muscle through it, though. I remember watching when he'd take a hit, seeing him hoist that shredded shoulder back into place, refusing to come out of the game. *Just call the next play.* That's the kind of toughness that kept him going. Weaker men would've never made it for as long as Brodie did.

But the body can only absorb so much punishment. After four or five pro seasons, he was done. And that was the end of all those long hours of practice drills and minicamps and two-a-days—the end of a little boy's imagination, out in the lengthening shadows of the side yard, scrambling to find a pretend receiver on the final drive, heaving the winning touchdown as the clock ticked down to zero.

The end. The end?

That's the end of it all? Seriously?

No, that's how the beer bellies see it, the ones who dope up on chili dogs and bratwurst in their oversized flannel shirts on Saturdays and Sundays in the fall, who don't understand that life is larger than football, not the other way around. Life wasn't over for Brodie when he retired from the NFL, playing for mostly bad teams through disappointing seasons on the field, fighting through injuries that limited what his natural ability was fully capable of doing.

No, that's not where hope dies.

Because the real Brodie was never wrapped up in what he *did*, just as the real you isn't wrapped up in what *you* do either. The real you is *who you are*. The real you is that person inside you that can't be defined by circumstances and events, by what happened in the past and by how it affected you. The real you is the person you're still growing into and becoming, the person who's constantly discovering what matters most in life, who's learning—through both the hard lessons and the little victories—exactly who you want to be with God's help.

And so we're back around now to Jesus' statements that I mentioned at the start of the chapter—how none of us can do anything *without* Him but how nothing is impossible *with* Him—how in the words of Proverbs 16:9, "A man's heart plans his way, but the LORD determines his steps."

That's why God could keep working in Brodie's heart and bring him back to the Ranch for whatever season of time the Lord chooses—because God's a real God, working in a real man who's much more than what he once did on a football field.

And that same real God still has work to do through the real you as well, no matter what's come along in your life to cloud that person from view, causing you to doubt whether he or she is even down there inside you anymore.

I mean, sure, what's taken place in your life is real. It happened. You did it. They said it. You started it. Whichever combination of pieces comes together to tell your story, they're real. And you can't deny they exist. I'm not *asking* you to deny them.

So, yes, you may need to do some apologizing. You may have some forgiving to do. You may need to turn off the television tonight and spend some time thinking through what could start you down a more hopeful road than the one you've been traveling on. And you may need some help to get you going because none of us is as strong by ourselves as we are when supported by others.

But whatever the realities and whatever they require, you can do it.

You can.

Because there's always hope.

Something to Hope For

Hopelessness, at its heart, is a lonely word. Sure, it may often be triggered and agitated by others, like the way many of our kids have been driven toward it through the demeaning negligence and indifference of their parents and family. But in order for hopelessness to attach itself to us and begin to define our outlook, it must convince us that we're disqualified from overcoming what we've done and what's been done to us, that we are the hopeless outliers in a whole world of people who are out there enjoying what we can never experience ourselves . . . simply because of who we are.

And that's simply not true.

If you're feeling discouraged and beat down today, it could be coming from anywhere. Perhaps it stems from shortcuts you've taken in your work ethic, from failures in staying true to your ideals and priorities, from financial problems and worries, from a compromise of your morals, from disharmony in your family and relationships. I don't know. Only *you* know. Whether it's from your own regrettable mistakes, the heartless actions of others, or simply the hard knocks of life, all the ingredients are in place for cooking up a scenario that looks too bleak and uninspiring to want to fight against much longer.

But if hopelessness is what you're feeling as a conclusion, it's because you've chosen to swallow down a batch of condemning lies, which nobody can force you to drink. And excuse me for saying so, but it usually includes a double shot of self-pity, to help make it go down a little easier.

It's a lie. A deception. Even self-deception.

Because hopelessness, as I said, is a lonely word. That's how it maintains its power base. That's the position it tries to capture and monopolize, blinding you from any other viewpoint than your own self-image.

What hopelessness doesn't want you to see is that so many other factors, if allowed to properly light the room, could shine enough different perspectives on what's there, you'd no longer feel like you're alone with no way out. That's why the best way to treat hopelessness is to be honest about what's brought it on, drag it out into the open, and then leave it there—leave it to go haunt some other poor sucker who's willing to believe its narrow view of life.

Maybe I'm a little rougher on this subject than I would ordinarily be, had God put me in a more traditional line of work. But if all we did at Big Oak Ranch was to swirl around in our own stew of problems all the time, our kids would never be able to see over the top of them. They've had enough terrible things happen to them, they could go around feeding the self-pity meter all day every day, and nobody would think they didn't deserve to. So, I mean, we're fine with talking honestly and openly about all kinds of hard things—and we do. But we don't see much point in peeling away layer after layer of the onion when we know we won't find anything at the center when we're finished . . . except more hopelessness. And that's just not something we wish to tame or tolerate around here. Hopelessness is something we intend to take behind the woodshed and beat the tar out of.

It doesn't play nice, and neither do we.

And so I want to leave you with a few challenges that will (hopefully) prevent that nagging sense of hopelessness from making you want to give up and quit, teasing you to lie down in its lap and fall for its lies.

To make these points a little more memorable, I've started them with the letters of the standard grading system at school— A, B, C, D, and F. And in this class any letter grade is a good one. Collect them all.

A: *Attitude.* You are *not* a worthless, washed-up, no-good piece of trash. You're not a quitter. You're not a loser. But if you head out into the day feeling pretty sure those descriptors are true, you'll end up making decisions and gravitating toward people that confirm your low conclusions about yourself. Bottom line: you are the person who gets to decide what your attitude is going to be, no matter what anyone else's loud opinion of you may be telling you. And since you're the one in charge of it, why not go out there and make it a good one?

B: *Backbone.* Today will present you with a number of different opportunities for managing your time, your money, your conscience, and your affections. Some of these opportunities coming up today—*many* of them, in fact—may involve some of the same kinds of decisions that have caused you to be down on yourself for not handling them well in the past. But remember, it's never too late to do the right thing. So shore up that desire for sticking to your principles. Even if you've goofed it up royally in times past, today calls for a backbone of steel. You'll feel a little more hopeful by nightfall if you do.

C: *Christ centered.* All this talk about tightening up our lives and striving to be the real us—let's not go all "believe in yourself" like a Family Channel movie, creating the misguided idea that we're capable of eradicating what's wrong with us all by our own bootstraps. The only successful life, like the only healthy heart, is the one that's fueled by faith in Jesus, trusting Him and being thankful to Him for blessings that outnumber even our most hopeless complaints. The gratitude part alone, if we'll learn to get that right, will go a long way toward quieting our inner cynic or critic.

D: *Determination.* The beautiful part about serving God is that He is so huge and eternal and can see everything all at once, our trust in Him is anchored in sheer bedrock. If we only knew the enormity of details He orchestrates for us behind the scenes—all while we're usually complaining about how inattentive, uncaring, and absent He is—we would be blown away. And we would never lack for hope. And yet, because of how He's designed our lives on Earth to work, He chooses to cooperate with our active will to bring about what He wants to do in us. So even in depending on Him completely, we also get to choose—to determine—how we're going to live. Do it with real purpose, resolve, and intention.

Finally—**F:** *Finish.* You and I, if we're choosing wisely, can do the A, B, C, D of this process pretty well. Good attitude. Strong backbone. Steady faith. Pure determination. But we've all seen enough people—athletes, celebrities, politicians, business whizzes—who took off like a ball of fire, but then they felt entitled, enamored by their success, into coasting for a little while. Didn't keep it up. Didn't finish.

When Jesus comes, or when we're safely home with Him at the end of our lives, we can kick back and rest at that point. That's our confirmed hope as Christians. But until then we've got a job to do. And anything that's worth *starting* well—or even anything we've started *not* so well—is still worthy of *finishing* well.

Because there's a whole lot to still be hopeful about.

Hope in Hard Places

When I was fifteen years old, my parents and I were up in New York State, visiting relatives. A howling blizzard had struck the area, but we were needing to head home. Being back at work and school the next week couldn't wait. We needed to go.

So we said our good-byes, trudged to the car, and prepared to leave, when my dad said, "OK, son, you're driving."

Me? No. Me? You mean me? The ink on my learner's permit had barely dried. I did good to keep the car on the road in good weather, on straight stretches, with clear visibility feeding me full information through every window and mirror.

"Frank?" my mom said, incredulous. "You're going to let him drive?"

"We've got to teach him," he said. "He can do it."

So with hands securely locked at ten and two, going about three miles an hour, with the wipers barely sweeping the snow from the windshield before the next pile could form, I drove us through to safety. Unbelievable. Thought I'd kill us all.

But my father was giving me confidence that I could do hard things. He was allowing me to go through a new experience that would later develop, in the midst of other hard experiences, into a deep-seated reservoir of hope.

I did something sort of similar with Brodie. He was a little younger, actually—maybe nine. We were out in the back pasture in our old stick-shift jeep. I cut the engine off, turned to him, and said, "OK, son, pretend Daddy just had a heart attack. Get me home."

Huh?

"Come on. Let me see you get me home."

"Uh, Dad, are you all right?"

"Yeah, I'm fine. But what if I wasn't? What would you do?"

OK. So he lugged me over onto the passenger side, climbed behind the wheel, revved the motor, and lurched it into gear, hardly able to press all the way down on the clutch without a full leg extension, but driving just the same. Got me out of there. And learned a great lesson.

I was giving him confidence. Giving him reason to hope.

And if you take anything away from the time you've spent in this book, I pray it will be a renewed sense of hope that whatever's happened, whatever your past has been like, however hard it's been and may continue to be, the most natural conclusion will be what perhaps seems the most illogical conclusion—that you have God, that you have ability, and that you have hope.

Being here at the Ranch all these years, I've asked God many times why He would allow our kids to endure what they've been through. The abuse they've taken, the blows they've received, the various struggles and seasons of failure they've been pushed into by people who were supposed to love and protect them. Why? Why would He let *anybody*—but especially these kids—be pockmarked with so many bad memories and hard experiences?

I've never really gotten a full answer—not because there *isn't* one but because my mind and heart are not capable of fully grasping and understanding. I'm sure, though, that a big part of the answer is because hope often grows most spectacularly in places that appear the most hopeless.

"Hope deferred makes the heart sick," the Bible says, "but desire fulfilled is a tree of life" (Prov. 13:12 NASB).

Or as I like to think of it—a Big Oak.

Just Be Yourself

"Tell me about your family," I asked him, this twelve-year-old boy in front of me. He and his little brother, age seven, had been brought to us for their protection.

"Well, they'd tell me sometimes to go get Danny here, to bring him over to where they were, and then they'd yell at him, push around on him, beat him."

"Beat him?"

"Yeah."

"And what did *you* do . . . while they were beating him?"

"I'd hold him down."

"Really?"

"Well, I mean, I'd lay on top of him. I'd cover him."

"You mean so they couldn't get to him?"

He smiled a faint but cagey grin. Didn't say anything at first. Just sat there remembering those violent moments when he was shielding his little brother with his own tenacious body. Tough guy, this kid was. And not even a teenager yet.

"It's no big deal," he finally said, stoically, hoping this answer would be the end of it.

"Let me see your back," I pressed him.

"It's OK. You don't need to do that."

"Yes, I do. Let me see it."

He got up, turned around, faced away from me, and lifted up his shirt. From his waist to his shoulder blades, up one side and down the other, his twelve-year-old back was one huge canvas of bruises, scar tissue, and infected scratches. His little brother's back, on the other hand, looked like it had never been touched. Because it hadn't. Because of him.

"It's no big deal," he said, tugging his shirt back down.

And yeah, I guess he's right. When you've got it—the "it" I was talking about when we first started—it's just *who you are.*

It's no big deal.

And as we wrap things up here, I just want to say: If this book has come off sounding like a lot of stuff to process and remember, if it's left you feeling as though you're way off-center and not really sure how to work yourself back, don't make the answer more of big deal than it really is. Let's just make this real simple.

I like simple.

One more story by way of illustration, and we're nearly done.

Studded into a small concrete monument at a place called Meades Ranch, an otherwise nondescript piece of acreage in Osborne, Kansas, is a simple bronze disk that marks what's called the geodetic base point of the United States. Basically it's dead center, geographically speaking, for the entire land mass that comprises the lower forty-eight, the contiguous states.

The reason they pressed the pin in the ground on that precise spot involved more than just yardstick math. It also involved other factors as well, like the curvature of the earth and other topological properties that are second nature to those who

understand physical science. But for most of the twentieth century, before fancy-smancy satellite imagery created adjustments
to the best human calculations of the late 1800s, this single
marker in northern Kansas served as the central reference for all
land survey measurements conducted throughout the U.S.

So the people who drew up plot maps and land deeds during all those years of our nation's history, when they wanted
to find out exactly where a piece of property stood in relation
to center, they didn't need to just guess. Nor did they need to
gather armfuls of information or take hundreds of other details
and observations into account before they could feel good about
it. Since every official land measurement was reckoned and syn-
chronized from that small, anchored disk, immovable out there
on the Midwestern plains, all they needed to do was to find their
distance from that one point. Start there, and you've got it.

And the same thing is true of you and me today.

We can know where true center lies and then build our lives
based on it.

Somebody like me can ask a lot of questions. I can ramble
on, as you see now, for nearly two hundred pages, and might
only succeed at making everything I say more muddled and
confusing than before I even started.

But there's a time to quit asking questions, and a time to just
sit down with some solid answers.

Time to make it simple.

And here, I believe, are the three basic, no-big-deal elements
that will help us make sense of all the things we've talked about
in this book, as well as the thousands of other decisions and
dilemmas that can crop up on any given day.

1. *Read your Bible.* According to Scripture, God says that we
are the sheep, and He is the Shepherd. And this amazing book
He's given us—which, depending on your history with it, may
seem either impossibly old and imposing or perhaps just far too
familiar to promise anything new to say—is our key gateway

to His voice, His direction. There's no set formula for how to read it, although if you ask around, people can share with you their own favorite method. The only one that doesn't work, I've found, is the one where you *don't read it*. So open it up every day, and let God speak His truth to you in His own words. You'll be stunned, again and again, how directly it applies to your life. And by turning its teaching into real, everyday faith and action, you'll stay centered in who God created you to be.

2. *Pray*. Prayer is simply honest, transparent conversation. I know it sounds like a monologue when you're doing it. But the Word of God promises—as impossible as the sheer physics seem to be—that He is actively listening and responding to each prayer, from each of His people, at any moment of the day or night. And if we will quit doing all our talking to ourselves and will turn it into actual, living, breathing prayers to an actual, living, eternal God—who isn't just *there* but who loves us with a Father's love—He will guide our hearts into the right places where He wants them to go, doing the things that He's made us to do.

3. *Trust the Holy Spirit*. If you're a believer in Christ, His Spirit is inside you, communicating the things of God to you in a manner that He allows us to understand. No, it's not the same kind of voice that we're accustomed to hearing from one another, the kind that goes into our ears (and usually out the other). It's just a . . . knowing. You just know. And through this simple but often overlooked strategy of reading the Bible and praying to its Author, this voice of His that seems so mysterious to us becomes more and more clear the more we do it and the better we listen.

He keeps drawing us back to center.

Back to who we are.

Back home.

Acknowledgments

There would be no Big Oak Ranch without the Lord's grace and loving-kindness. We are forever indebted to His children that He has put in our care, who taught us the true meaning of "Who You Are."

Special thanks to Lawrence Kimbrough for capturing the stories and experiences from four decades of raising children and making them come to life.